·····— JOHN LOECKE'S —·····

GROSGRAIN STYLE

JOHN LOECKE'S

GROSGRAIN STYLE

QUICK AND CREATIVE PROJECTS FOR ACCESSORIZING
AND DECORATING WITH GROSGRAIN RIBBON

PHOTOGRAPHY BY
WENDELL WEBBER

POTTER CRAFT

NEW YORK

Copyright © 2007 by John Loecke
Photography copyright © 2007 by Wendell Webber

Published in the United States by Potter Craft, an imprint of the Crown
Publishing Group, a division of Random House, Inc., New York.
www.crownpublishing.com
www.pottercraft.com

POTTER CRAFT and CLARKSON N. POTTER are trademarks, and
POTTER and colophon are registered trademarks of Random House, Inc.

Library of Congress Cataloging-in-Publication Data
Loecke, John.
John Loecke's grosgrain style : quick and creative projects for
accessorizing and decorating with grosgrain ribbon /
photography by Wendell Webber. — 1st ed.
p.   cm.
Includes bibliographical references and index.
ISBN 978-0-307-34551-6
1. Ribbon work.   2. House furnishings.   I. Title.
TT850.5.L64   2007
646.2'1—dc22   2007002662

Printed in China

Design by Amy Sly

1 3 5 7 9 10 8 6 4 2

First Edition

ACKNOWLEDGMENTS

This book would not have been possible without the help of many talented people, including: KRISTINE KENNEDY, my editor at *Better Homes and Gardens,* who suggested that I do this book; ROSEMARY NGO and CHRISTINA SCHOEN, my editors at Potter Craft; CARLA GLASSER, my agent; WENDELL WEBBER, my photographer; BECKY MAYER and her team of talented seamstresses in Urbandale, Iowa; GARY SIMMONS, whose Mountain Brook Inn in Bovina, New York, is the setting for the room in the "Let the Games Begin" chapter; and DAWN BARR, who graciously volunteered to model my ribbon aprons.

Thanks also to my partner, JASON OLIVER NIXON, who, despite overseeing a major home renovation, helped road-test all the creations. And last but not least, a big Thank-You to my Mom, MARLENE LOECKE, who helped create and craft all the projects you see in this book.

CONTENTS

CHAPTERONE
LIVELY LIVING SPACES

CHAPTERTWO
SLEEP BRIGHT

CHAPTERTHREE
LET THE GAMES BEGIN

CHAPTER FOUR
RECIPE FOR A COLORFUL KITCHEN

CHAPTER FIVE
DINING BY DESIGN

CHAPTER SIX
ALL DECKED OUT

WHY RIBBON?

I have always been fascinated with the many decorative uses of ribbon—especially grosgrain. My grandmother, who used it religiously every time she wrapped gifts, first introduced me to this wondrous embellishment. She had a secret stash in the basement that, to a small child, seemed to encompass every color of the rainbow. She amassed this collection by shopping holiday sales and closeouts and hitting every trim store she passed in her travels. She also saved every snippet—striped, polka-dot, and otherwise patterned—that she received. If a store wrapped up her purchase with a tidy grosgrain ribbon bow, you could be assured that the ribbon, no matter what the color or pattern, would find its way into her stash.

As I grew older, I came to learn that grosgrain could be used for more than merely tying pretty bows around packages. I learned—in part, from my grandmother—that it could be worn as a belt (the back of her closet door was filled with hooks, each one holding a belt made from a different ribbon pattern), wrapped around a lampshade, or used to dress up plain curtains and chair covers.

Today I follow my grandmother's lead. My closet is overflowing with ribbon belts of every color. And every time I go in a store, I have my packages wrapped, just so I can undo the grosgrain ribbon that closes the box when I get home. I'm obsessed, yes, but to me, there's no better embellishment than grosgrain. Why? It's synthetic and durable (read: machine washable and sturdy), pliable, and available in a wide assortment of colors and patterns. What's more, it's accessible (easy to find on the shelves of your corner craft store) and relatively inexpensive, depending on the amount required. The crosswise rib can take a beating and, unlike a delicate silk or sheer ribbon, still look great. And because grosgrain is such a hardy choice, it can be tossed in the washing machine—a real bonus if, like me, you use it to trim everything from table linens to towels. But the real reason I favor grosgrain is that this simple staple is available in so many vibrant colors and patterns—pink and green stripes, yellow polka dots, rich chocolate browns. With so many color and pattern choices, the decorating possibilities are practically endless.

In fact, I am so obsessed with this preppy embellishment that I allowed its simple charms to influence my choice of careers. Back in college, a friend, interested in giving her bland apartment some fashionable flair, asked me for advice on turning plain cotton curtain panels into show-stopping window treatments. I suggested trimming the panels in a latticelike pattern of pink and green grosgrain. She loved the idea, and so did all her friends. Before I knew it, I was not only designing dorm rooms, I was also studying the finer points of furniture placement and color theory.

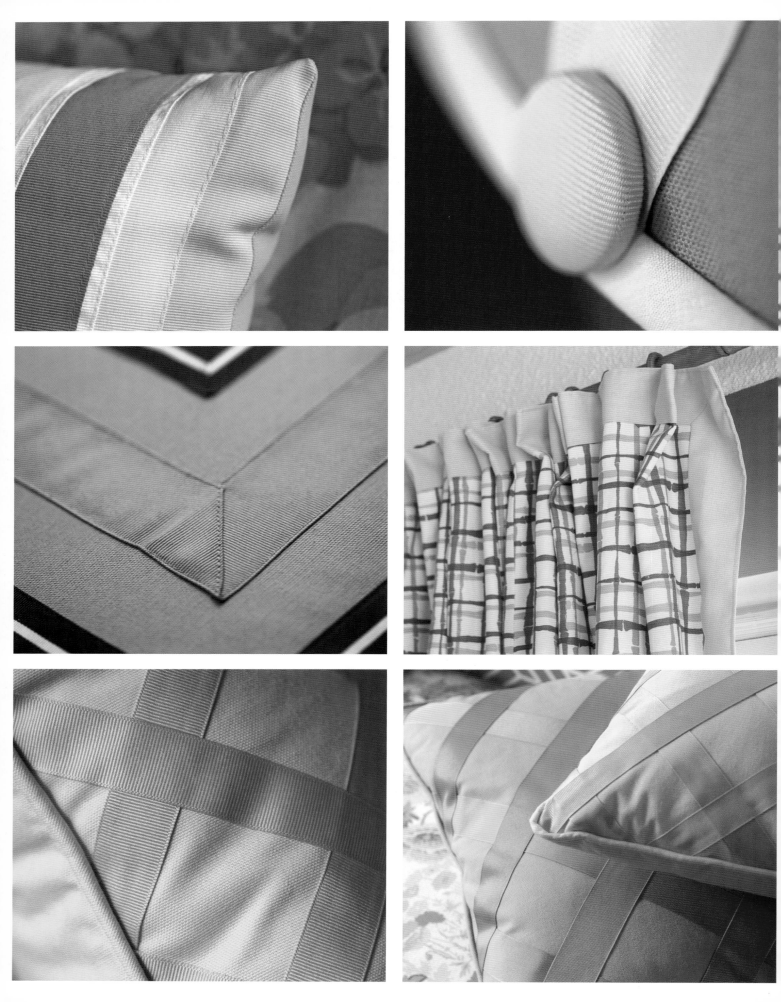

To this day, grosgrain is a staple in my arsenal of decorative tricks, and when a private client hires me to design a room, more often than not it will end up with some type of grosgrain embellishment, be it a pillow, a lampshade, or even a simple covered box. Recently, a client asked me to design a light and airy sunroom—"a space," she said, "that feels like summer year round, but doesn't have the usual mix of rattan furniture and tropical plants." My answer was to fill the room with overstuffed sofas and chairs covered in bright floral prints accented by—you guessed it—contrasting colors of grosgrain ribbon. I started simply by adding pillows with a latticelike ribbon pattern. She was so elated with the result that I added grosgrain trims to each of the lampshades, the buttons on the backs of a few tufted chairs, and the seats of several others.

Before you get started, take a moment and flip through the pages of this book. I hope the ideas presented here will be a springboard for your own creativity. Though I've categorized the individual projects by room, feel free to mix and match. For example, the treatment that I used for pillows on my bed might look divine on chairs in your dining room. Similarly, the floral pattern I used on my kitchen apron could easily be adapted to the face of a pillow.

Because this book is meant to inspire, I've also kept instructions to a minimum. What's more, almost everything in the book can be replicated in usable fashion with little or no sewing. That's right, you read correctly—no sewing. The secret lies in a new craft material called Sealah tape, a double-sided, pressure-sensitive adhesive that holds like glue without the mess.

Bottom line: Use your imagination. Have fun. There's nothing I love better than discovering a new way to use ribbon.

CHAPTER 1

Lively Living Spaces

COFFEE TABLES · PILLOWS · LAMPSHADES ·

WHILE IT'S TRUE THAT THE BEAUTY of grosgrain ribbon has always fascinated me, my conversion to using it as a decorative element in my home came about largely by chance when I decided to "redo" my hand-me-down living room sofa. The sofa in question, a classic Chippendale-style two-seater with nubby brown fabric and a seat cushion of blue polished cotton, did nothing for my freshly painted pale-green living room. The sofa had presence, but it lacked personality. Of course, once I finished trimming the sofa cushions in grosgrain, I was hooked. Next, I embellished the drapes ($30 cotton panels that I picked up at a discount store) with a jaunty grid of criss-crossed blue, brown, and green ribbons; added a hint of ribbon to the lampshades; decorated the top of the coffee table; and, after some practice, made an area rug. And that's the lesson here: Creating rooms that look like they belong in the pages of a decorating magazine doesn't require tons of cash. Rather, it requires a little ingenuity and the ability to look at the things you already own with a fresh eye.

COFFEE TABLES

Coffee tables often fall front-and-center in a living room furniture arrangement. To that end they should be attention grabbing. Give your table a fashion-forward look by outlining the edge in ribbons that coordinate with your room's color scheme. For this table, I designed the pattern so that it falls on the top, but you can also run ribbon around the sides of the table or down the legs.

MATERIALS

Coffee table

Gloss paint

Mod Podge or polyurethane

Sealah tape

Burnishing tool

Ribbon

String

Scissors

Paintbrush

NOTE Ribbon quantities depend on table dimensions. To determine the quantity of ribbon you'll need, lay out a pattern with string and measure. The table shown left uses approximately 7 yards (6.4m) of ribbon.

INSTRUCTIONS

Let the shape of your table's top dictate the arrangement of your ribbons.

Once you've determined your pattern (I selected a rectangular design that contrasted nicely with my table's scalloped edge), secure the ribbon to the top surface with Sealah tape and the burnishing tool.

Finish and protect the ribbon by covering the entire tabletop with a coat of Mod Podge or polyurethane.

SOURCE TIP I started this project with an old table that I picked up at a garage sale for $15. Because the table's finish was brown and far from pristine, I decided to refinish it first with a fresh coat of gloss white paint.

PILLOWS

Pillows are an easy way to bring color into a room without drastically altering the overall look. Have fun. Mix patterns and sizes. Play up a secondary color in your decorating scheme. Use unusual store-bought finds or create your own. Regardless, add an extra flourish by embellishing them with ribbon.

MATERIALS

Patterned or solid fabric (you should be able to cut one 24-inch [61cm] square pillow from 1 yard of 54-inch [137cm] wide decorator fabric)

Ready-made pillow form (available at craft stores)

Ribbon

Sealah tape

Burnishing tool

Sewing needle

Thread in color that matches fabric

NOTE Ribbon quantity depends on the pattern and size of the finished pillow. The animal-print pillow took approximately 3 yards (2.7m) of green ribbon and 3 yards (2.7m) of brown ribbon. The lattice pillow called for approximately 5 yards (4.6m) of cream ribbon.

INSTRUCTIONS

Cut two panels of fabric to the size required to cover a standard pillow form, adding ¼ inch (6mm) of seam allowance to each side of each panel.

Affix the ribbon to the fabric squares with Sealah tape before sewing the squares together. This way, if your pattern extends to the very edge of the pillow (like the lattice pillow pictured left), you can hide the ends of the ribbon in the seam.

Once your pattern is secure, turn the panels so the right sides are facing and pin them together, making sure the seams match up. Sew together, leaving one side open.

Turn right side out. Insert the pillow form and hand-stitch the opening closed or insert a zipper. If sewing isn't an option, Sealah tape and a burnishing tool can also be used to affix ribbon to the face of a ready-made shape. Your pattern will simply be limited to the center of the pillow's face.

COLOR TIP When selecting ribbons to enhance your pillows, look for designs that contrast with the color of the pillow fabric. For example, solid oranges, greens, and yellows look great on shades of blue. Take the opposite approach when adding ribbon to a patterned fabric. Determine the most prominent colors and then look for ribbons that share those hues.

LAMPSHADES

Lampshades, by their very nature, are a decorative element meant to disguise something that isn't so pretty. Isn't it strange, then, that they are often so uninspiring? Fortunately, they don't have to be. With a yard of fabric, coordinating ribbon, and some glue, you can give an ordinary shade a designer look.

MATERIALS

Plain paper shade or hard-backed linen shade

Brown mailing paper

Fabric

Aleene's No-Sew fabric glue

Paintbrush

Ribbon

Sealah tape

Burnishing tool

NOTE Ribbon quantity will depend on the size of your shade and the pattern you wish to create. The shade shown right used approximately 3 yards (2.7m) of ribbon.

INSTRUCTIONS

Inspect your lamp's existing shade. If it's a plain paper or other hard-backed style, you're in business. If not, you will first need to purchase a shade.

Next, select a fabric and ribbons that coordinate with the color of your lamp base. Make a pattern for cutting the fabric by rolling the lampshade across a large piece of brown mailing paper, tracing the shape as you go. Use this pattern to cut the fabric to fit the shade.

Adhere the fabric to the shade using Aleene's No-Sew fabric glue (it won't bleed through the material). Affix the ribbon to the shade with Sealah tape and the burnishing tool, or fabric glue. For a simpler design that saves a step, skip the fabric cover and simply secure ribbon to the plain shade.

SIZE TIP A lampshade should look proportional to the base on which it sits; as a rule of thumb, the shade for a table lamp should be at least two-thirds the height of the base. The shade should also be wide enough to allow at least a 2-inch (5cm) separation between the bulb and the shade on all sides and long enough to cover the electrical fittings.

CURTAIN PANELS

Ready-made curtain panels can be turned into custom drapes with the simple addition of colorful grosgrain layered in an eye-catching pattern. Solid panels are a safe bet, but a simple pattern like stripes or checks can also be used to make a plain room pop. Whichever you choose, you'll be amazed at the compliments showered on you for your decorating savvy.

MATERIALS

Ready-made curtain panels in a color or pattern that matches your room's décor

Ribbon

Scissors

Fabric tape measure

Sealah tape

Burnishing tool

NOTE Ribbon quantity will depend on the size of your curtain panels and the pattern you wish to create. For the 84-inch (213cm) panels shown left, I used approximately 13 yards (12m) of wide green ribbon, 10 yards (9.1m) of wide brown and cream ribbon, 18 yards (16.5m) of dark brown ribbon, 16 yards (14.6m) of pale blue ribbon, and 2 yards (1.8m) of polka-dot ribbon for the tabs.

INSTRUCTIONS

Ready-made curtain panels are sold in standard lengths (72" [183cm], 84" [213cm], and 96" [244cm] lengths are the most common). Begin by selecting the size that fits your windows.

Next, choose ribbons in colors and patterns that fit the look of your room. For example, if many of the furnishings in your room are in shades of brown, cream, green, and blue, then look for grosgrain in the same colors. Adding a patterned ribbon to the mix (like the brown-on-brown polka-dot grosgrain that I used for the tabs) can help give your panels a more relaxed look. For interest, select ribbons of varying width, and layer narrower ribbons over wider ones.

Lay out your pattern first, then affix the ribbons to the fabric with Sealah tape and the burnishing tool.

PLANNING TIP

Don't waste ribbon. Instead, sketch out possible panel patterns on a piece of paper, using a different color pencil or marker for each type of ribbon you want to use. When you arrive at a design you like, calculate the amount of grosgrain you need by counting the lines of the same color and multiplying by the length or width of the panel, depending on the direction in which the ribbon runs.

RUGS

Rugs are a practical and pretty way to soften hardwood floors. They can also be used, as shown on pages 12 and 13, to define a seating area in the living room. But why settle for an ordinary wool rug when you can make a real style statement with a rug fashioned from ribbon. And lest you think ribbon belongs on wrapping paper and not wood floors, think again. This simple craft store staple is sturdy and machine washable.

MATERIALS

Sailcloth

Scissors

Ribbon

Sewing machine

Thread in color(s) that complement ribbon

NOTE Ribbon quantity will depend on the size of the rug and the pattern you wish to create. For the 4 feet x 5 feet (1.2mx1.5m) rugs shown left, I used approximately 10 yards (9.1m) of ribbon. Four colors of ribbon were used so you would need approximately 5 yards (4.6m) of each color to make one rug.

INSTRUCTIONS

Determine the size of the rug you want to make. 3 feet x 5 feet (.9mx1.5m), 5 feet x 7 feet (1.5mx2.13m), and 8 feet x 10 feet (2.4mx3m) are standard. Then cut a piece of sailcloth to those dimensions.

Select ribbons and lay out the pattern on the sailcloth. (To copy the design shown left, you will need four colors and two widths of grosgrain.)

Beginning at one end, lay down the first ribbon. Secure it to the fabric by stitching down the inside edge. Hide the stitching by overlapping the second ribbon ¼ inch (6mm). Repeat until the sailcloth is completely covered.

Finish the edges of the longest sides by turning back ribbon ends and running a continuous stitch down the length of the rug.

SIZE TIP The larger your rug, the more cumbersome it will be to run through the sewing machine. If you'd like to make an 8 feet x 10 feet (2.4mx3m) rug, make four 4 feet x 5 feet (1.2mx 1.5m) rugs instead, then sew them together by hand, or simply layer them on the floor.

BLINDS

Blinds help shield your home's interior from prying eyes. They also shield fabrics and furnishings from unwanted exposure to the sun. You can make these utilitarian window treatments as stylish as the rest of your home by trimming the colored tapes that disguise the mechanisms that make them function with a contrasting color of ribbon.

MATERIALS

Ribbon in color that contrasts with tape of blind

Small paintbrush

Aleene's No-Sew fabric glue

INSTRUCTIONS

Select a ribbon that is narrower in width than the fabric tape on the blind. Here, I used a ½ inch (13mm) ribbon since the tape on my blind measured 1 inch (2.5cm).

Cut the ribbon to fit the length of the blind.

Apply a thin coat of fabric glue to the back of the ribbon and press the ribbon to the tape.

COLOR TIP   When selecting a contrasting ribbon, consider the color of your drapes. Perhaps pick a ribbon that incorporates an accent color from the drapes and use that to highlight the tape on the blind.

Sleep Bright

BEDDING · HEAD- AND FOOTBOARDS · NIGHTSTANDS

SATISFIED WITH MY HANDIWORK in the living room—and beaming with many compliments from family and friends—I couldn't be stopped. I turned my attention to transforming my bedroom, a place where I could further show off my love for blue and green. Several years ago, while working as a new-product editor for several home magazines, I came across a very expensive set of designer sheets with impeccable grosgrain detailing. One look at the blue-and-white-striped trim and I was in heaven, but the sheets, of course, were not in my budget. I did, however, make note of the idea (I carry a notebook with me everywhere for this very reason) and filed it away. Here—at long last—was my opportunity to finally use that idea. Of course, I didn't stop with the sheets. Rather, I created a complete bed set—duvet, pillow shams and decorative toss pillows, bed skirt, and head- and footboard covers. I also embellished the nightstands, picture frames, and other decorative elements in the room. Talk about starting the day in a bright way!

BEDDING

Bedding is to beds what clothing is to the body. Without it, the bed would be naked. Sheets, pillowcases, and even comforters can be found for little money at discount and department stores, but why settle for the ordinary? Instead, enhance your basic bed linens with ribbon. And because there's no rule that says every piece of bedding must match, you should feel free to use ribbons in a variety of colors, patterns, and widths. That is, after all, the hot look.

MATERIALS

Solid or patterned bedding

Ribbon

Pins

Sealah tape

Burnishing tool

Sewing needle

Thread in colors that complement ribbon

NOTE Ribbon quantities depend on the pattern you choose. For example, to create the checked pillow shams shown left, I used approximately 10 yards (9.1m) of ribbon. Adding stripes to a standard reversible queen duvet requires approximately 85 yards (78m) of ribbon.

INSTRUCTIONS

Select bedding and wash it. Lay out individual pieces on a large flat surface and experiment with different ribbon arrangements. When you come up with a design you like, pin the ribbon in place and attach it to the bedding with Sealah tape and the burnishing tool.

For bedding that you plan to sleep on (pillowcases and flat sheets, for example) designs are best kept to the outer edges to minimize wear. For decorative pillows and duvets, this is less of an issue. Remember, grosgrain is machine washable.

DESIGN TIP

There are numerous ways in which grosgrain can be used to turn a bland pillowcase into something special. The easiest, of course, is to apply the ribbon as a border several inches (centimeters) in from the edge of the pillow. Slightly more complicated, but equally pleasing, are graphic touches like grids, stripes, or diagonals. Bows, rosettes, and medallions lend a frilly, more feminine look.

HEAD- AND FOOTBOARD COVERS

Adding head- and footboard covers is a stylish way to give an old bed a new look. Like a slipcover for a sofa or chair, these custom fabric covers are designed to fit snuggly over the bed's existing upholstered frame, or they can be loosely draped over one made of metal. Here, the combination of a graphic print with contrasting ribbon lends a modern twist to an otherwise traditional room.

MATERIALS

Brown mailing paper

Fabric

Ribbon

Sewing machine (for slipcover only)

Sewing needle

Thread in color to coordinate with fabric

Sealah tape

Burnishing tool

Zipper

NOTE Ribbon quantities depend on the pattern you choose. To create the head- and footboard covers shown left, I used approximately 10 yards (9.1m) of ribbon.

INSTRUCTIONS

Trace an outline of both the headboard and the footboard onto brown mailing paper, adding ¼ inch (6mm) to the top and side edges for the seam allowance and adding ¼ inch (6mm) to the bottom for the hem.

Cut the fabric following the pattern.

Select ribbons in colors that complement those found in the fabric.

Lay out the ribbon and secure with Sealah tape or needle and thread. Turn the panels so the right sides are facing and pin them together, making sure the seams match up.

Sew together one side and the top, leaving one side open. Turn right side out. Add a zipper to the open side and hem the bottom.

CONSTRUCTION TIP

Ribbons also make effective fastenings, and ribbon ties are simpler than inserting zippers for closing a headboard cover. To add ribbon closures, stitch pairs of grosgrain strands (each about 6 inches [15cm] in length) into the seams of the open side. Once the cover is over the headboard, pull it tight and tie the ribbons into bows. Repeat for the footboard.

NIGHTSTANDS

Nightstands are a practical way to keep lamps, reading material, and other necessities in close proximity to the bed. But just because a nightstand is utilitarian doesn't mean that it has to be plain and simple. On the contrary, you can easily add pizzazz with a variety of patterned and solid ribbons.

MATERIALS

Nightstand

Ribbon

Sealah tape

Burnishing tool

Mod Podge or polyurethane

Paintbrush

Scissors

INSTRUCTIONS

Select a variety of ribbons that coordinate with the other colors in your room.

Let the shape of the nightstand determine the arrangement of the ribbons. For example, because the top of the stand shown left is square, I layered the ribbons in a patchwork fashion.

Affix the ribbon to the stand using Sealah tape and the burnishing tool.

Cover the top of the stand, or wherever you added ribbon, with several coats of Mod Podge or polyurethane to seal and protect the finish.

FINISHING TIP If your ribbon embellishment is not meant to be permanent, the ribbon can also be attached using double-sided tape.

MEDALLION LAMPSHADES

Medallions are the perfect way to use up small scraps of ribbon. Their whimsical shape adds texture and character to a room's overall design. Glue them to a lampshade, as I did here, or attach them to other objects in the space. With your imagination and a little hot glue, the possibilities are endless.

MATERIALS

Lampshade
Brown mailing paper
Fabric
Paintbrush
Aleene's No-Sew fabric glue
Grosgrain medallions
(I used twenty.)
Glue gun

INSTRUCTIONS

Inspect your lamp's existing shade. If it's a plain paper or other hard-backed style, you're in business. If not, you will first need to purchase a shade.

Make a pattern for cutting the fabric by rolling the lampshade across a large piece of brown mailing paper, tracing the shape as you roll.

Next, select a fabric that coordinates with the color of your lamp base.

Use the pattern to cut the fabric to fit the shade. Adhere the fabric to the shade using a paintbrush and Aleene's No-Sew fabric glue (it won't bleed through the fabric).

Make medallions (instructions on page 112) from ribbons that complement the fabric you selected. Use a glue gun to attach the medallions to the shade in a random fashion.

NOTE For a simpler design, simply secure the medallions to a plain shade without first covering it with fabric.

PLACEMENT TIP Although I created a random pattern when placing the medallions on the shade shown right, you can take the opposite approach and create a more formal look by lining them up at the shade's top and bottom edges.

BREAKFAST TRAYS

Breakfast trays, a throwback to simpler times, are a nice idea in today's hectic world. They can often be found at tag sales and secondhand shops. Spruce one up with ribbon, then use it to surprise a loved one with breakfast in bed.

MATERIALS

Breakfast tray

Paint

Paintbrushes

Ribbon

Scissors

Sealah tape

Burnishing tool

Mod Podge or polyurethane

INSTRUCTIONS

Revive an old tray with a fresh coat of paint.

Select ribbons that coordinate with the tray's new color.

When the paint is dry, lay out the pattern on the tray (I let the scallop shape of this tray's edges inspire my design) and secure the ribbons with Sealah tape and the burnishing tool.

Cover the tray with several coats of Mod Podge or polyurethane to make cleanup easy and to protect the ribbon from spills.

BUYING TIP

If you are patient, it's possible to find a vintage tray at a tag sale, flea market, or thrift shop. I found this one at a rummage sale for $10. However, if you can't wait to experience the pleasure of having breakfast in bed, you should be able to find a new, more streamlined design in the unfinished wood aisle of your local craft store.

PICTURE FRAMES

Picture frames are a necessity for displaying photographs and artwork. But sometimes a solid-color frame can feel too serious for what's inside. In these instances, lighten the look by adding ribbon to the face of the frame, to the mat around the picture, or to both.

MATERIALS

Picture frame
Ribbon
Sealah tape
Burnishing tool
Scissors

INSTRUCTIONS

Select ribbon that is narrower in width than the face of the frame you are covering. If the piece inside the frame has color—a picture of flowers, for example—choose ribbons that coordinate with those colors. Another option: Select ribbons that complement the color of the mat inside the frame.

Adhere the ribbon to the frame's face with Sealah tape and use the burnishing tool to press the ribbon in place. For a playful look, layer solid and patterned ribbons.

DESIGN TIP If your frame is too narrow to accommodate ribbon, switch gears and place the ribbon inside the frame. Use Sealah or double-sided tape to attach ribbon to the area of the mat that is visible through the glass.

Let the Games Begin

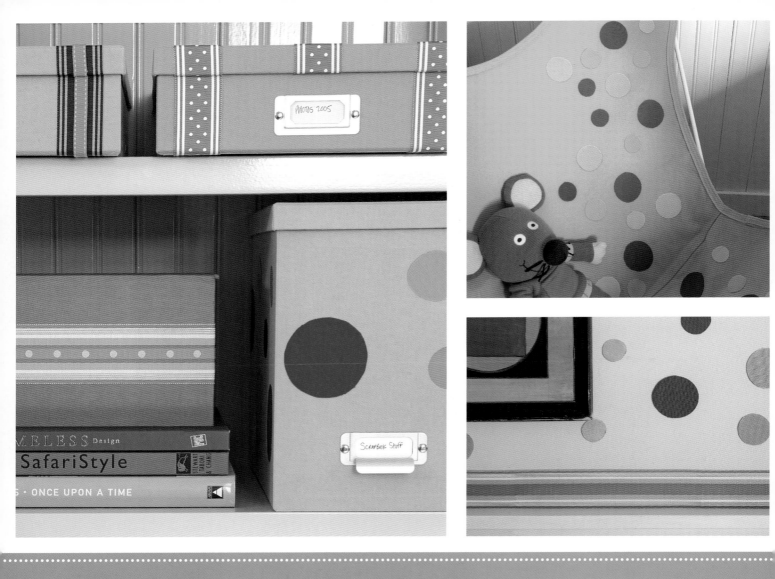

BUTTERFLY CHAIRS • WALL TREATMENTS

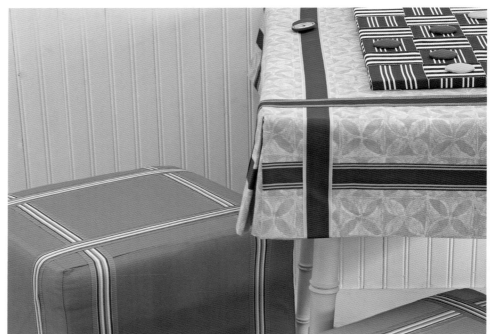

WHILE I DON'T HAVE CHILDREN of my own, I am, in many ways, a kid at heart. I also spent five years as the home editor of *Parents* magazine, a stint that taught me one very important thing: Kids love rooms filled with color and creative ideas. So, when a friend asked me to design a playroom for her two small boys, ages four and six, I knew exactly where to begin. Working with a palette that incorporated the boys' favorite colors (orange and blue), I designed a space that pops with personality. Mom was surprised at my choice of grosgrain as a major decorative element (it's on the walls, seating, storage containers, and even a giant-size checkerboard), but, as I explained, ribbon is adaptable. With a few minor tweaks (the grosgrain polka dots on the wall are removable), this room can look much more grownup.

NOTE TO PARENTS: Projects made with grosgrain are perfectly safe for children to handle. If, however, you are concerned that your child will pull off the ribbon, make sure you secure it in place with a permanent adhesive, like Sealah tape, or by sewing the ribbon to the object it will embellish.

BUTTERFLY CHAIRS

Butterfly chairs are a simple and inexpensive seating option for play spaces. Of course, they can look a little utilitarian, but that's easily remedied with an eye-popping grosgrain polka-dot design made from contrasting colors of ribbon.

MATERIALS

Butterfly chair

Ribbon in a variety of colors, patterns, and widths

Peel 'n' Stick paper

Scissors

X-acto knife

Circle templates or jar lids to trace

NOTE The adhesive on Peel 'n' Stick paper is not washable. If you want to be able to wash your chair cover, you will need to cut circles from ribbon and secure them in place using Sealah tape or a needle and thread.

INSTRUCTIONS

Select ribbons of varying width (we used 3-inch [7.6cm] for the largest circles, 2-inch [5cm] for the medium, and 1-inch [2.5cm] for the smallest) that coordinate with the color of your butterfly chair cover.

Remove the backing from one side of Peel 'n' Stick paper and lay down the ribbon.

Turn the paper over, trace circles, and cut them out.

Lay out the circles in random fashion on the chair cover.

When you're ready to apply them, score the back side with the X-acto knife and peel off the paper. Press the circles in place.

CIRCLE TIP

Peel 'n' Stick paper works better than Sealah tape to make any size circle because it comes in big sheets instead of different widths. However, Sealah tape can be substituted for paper if you don't mind the size limitations. Sealah tape also requires an extra step. To prevent fraying, circles made with Sealah tape should have their edges sealed with craft glue as described on page 115.

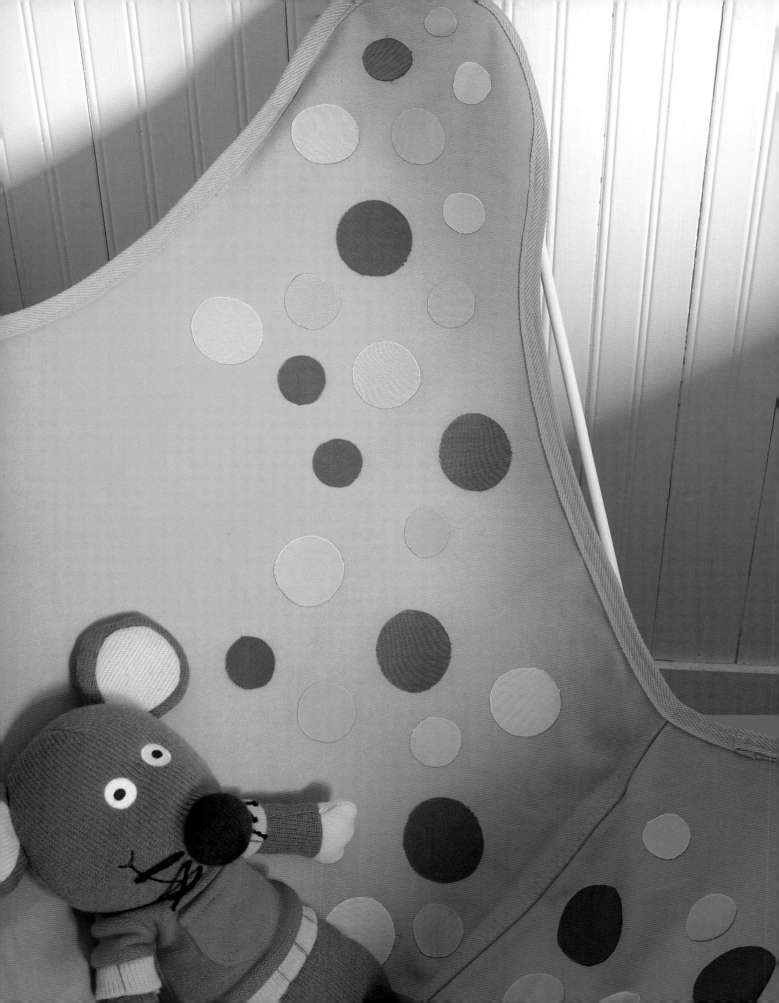

OTTOMANS

Ottomans are ideal kid-size seats. Not only are they readily available in a variety of sizes and price ranges, they are also supersoft and generally tip-free. When dressed in a bold fabric cover trimmed in a lively patterned grosgrain, this humble seat suddenly takes on a stylish appearance that will be welcome in any room of the house.

MATERIALS

Brown mailing paper

Ribbon

Sealah tape

Burnishing tool

Scissors

Pins

Sewing machine (to make slipcover)

NOTE Ribbon quantities depend on your ottoman's dimensions. To determine the amount of ribbon needed before beginning your project, lay out the pattern with string and measure it.

INSTRUCTIONS

Make a paper template of the ottoman's four sides and top, adding a ¼-inch (6mm) seam allowance for each edge.

Cut the fabric, turn the panels so the right sides are facing, and then pin them together, making sure the seams match up.

Sew the pieces together, adding one side at a time. Turn the cover right side out and place it over the ottoman.

Lay out the ribbon, cut, and secure it using Sealah tape. Use the burnishing tool to press the ribbon permanently in place.

PATTERN TIP Ribbon patterns can be varied by using diagonal lines or by having some strands run longer and others shorter. Another option is to layer a narrow patterned ribbon over the top of a wider solid ribbon.

GAME BOARDS

Game boards are readily available, but why settle for something run-of-the-mill when you can craft one from ribbon that's sure to become a family heirloom? A checkerboard, like the one shown right, can be easily constructed using two different kinds of ribbon. Complete the look by making ribbon-covered buttons that can be used for game pieces.

MATERIALS

One 24-inch (61cm) square piece of ¾-inch (19mm) plywood

Sandpaper

7 yards (6.4m) each of two 3-inch (7.6cm) wide ribbons

Staple gun using no smaller than ¼-inch (6mm) staples

Twenty-four 1-inch (2.5cm) buttons

1½ yards (1.4m) each of two 2-inch (5cm) wide ribbons in two contrasting colors

INSTRUCTIONS

Use the sandpaper to sand the edges of the plywood board until they are smooth.

Select two 3-inch (7.6cm) ribbons—one to run vertically and the other to run horizontally.

Take the ribbon that will run vertically and cut eight 28-inch (71cm) long strips.

Cover the entire board with these vertical strips, laying them so their edges touch but don't overlap. Attach the ribbon to the back of the board by pulling the ends to the back and stapling.

Cut eight 28-inch (71cm) long strips of ribbon and weave them through the vertical strips already attached to the board. Secure the strips to the board by stapling.

To make playing pieces, cover 1-inch (2.5cm) buttons with ribbon, making twelve buttons one color and twelve buttons another color.

SIZE TIP   To create a different size board, simply change the width of the ribbon. For example, use a 2-inch wide ribbon for a smaller board that measures 16 inches (40cm) square.

PHOTOS 2004

PHOTOS 2005

TIMELESS Design

SafariStyle

SLIM AARONS · ONCE UPON A TIME

Scrapbook Stuff

houseb

seductivebea

House + Garden

ELLE DECOR

MARTHA
LIV

STORAGE BOXES

Storage boxes, which can be found in a variety of bold colors and many different sizes, are must-have accessories for the playroom. And while their primary purpose is to help maintain order by housing toys, games, and craft supplies, they can also enhance the room's décor. Simply accessorize them with eye-popping ribbon trims.

MATERIALS

Cloth-covered storage boxes in a variety of sizes

Sealah tape

Burnishing tool

Ribbon in a variety of widths

Peel 'n' Stick paper

Scissors

X-acto knife

Circular templates or jar lids to trace

INSTRUCTIONS

Select storage boxes and ribbons that coordinate with the color of your room.

Experiment by layering ribbon over the box until you arrive at a pleasing pattern. Use Sealah tape to affix the ribbon to the box.

Press with the burnishing tool to adhere the ribbon permanently.

For polka-dot-covered boxes, select ribbons of varying width (I used 3-inch [7.6cm] for the largest circles, 2-inch [5cm] for the medium, and 1-inch [2.5cm] for the smallest) that coordinate with the color of your box.

Remove the backing from one side of the Peel 'n' Stick paper and lay down the ribbon. Turn the paper over, trace circles, and cut them out.

Lay out the circles in a random fashion on the box. When you're ready to apply them, score the back side with the X-acto knife and peel off the paper. Press in place.

DESIGN TIP

There are lots of storage containers to which ribbon can be affixed—canvas bins (available at places like the Container Store and Lowe's), wooden boxes, even wicker baskets, to name just a few. I happen to be partial to linen-covered boxes from russell+hazel available in a variety of striking colors. Mix and match, or choose a hue that complements your room's décor.

APRONS • SHELF LINERS • CANISTERS

AM A BIG BELIEVER IN THE IDEA that hardworking rooms, like kitchens, can—and should—have just as much style as the rest of the rooms in a house. So adding ribbon to the kitchen was a natural next step in my strategy to give my home décor a little pep. I started with the china hutch, a functional focal-point piece in need of a little zing. Ribbon, used as both an edge treatment on the shelves and an accent on the cabinet's beadboard back, did the trick. Now, you can't help but notice the cabinet and the delightful collection of dishes it holds. (For interest, I selected ribbons in colors that contrasted with the blues and greens of the dishes.) After doing the same to the island, I turned my attention to linens and storage containers—two things that could easily be mixed and matched, depending on my mood. And though grosgrain may seem like an odd choice for decorating an apron or towel that is sure to become soiled, it's not. The reason? Grosgrain is machine washable.

NOTE Because kitchens can be messy places, be sure that the ribbon you use for these projects is colorfast and can, therefore, stand up to washing (see page 116).

APRONS

Aprons are practical necessities in hardworking kitchens. Of course, practical doesn't mean that they can't be pretty. On the contrary, a plain apron may be purchased and trimmed with a colorful ribbon motif, like the sprightly daisy design shown left.

MATERIALS

Ready-made apron

Ribbon

Sewing needle

Thread in colors that coordinate with ribbon

Scissors

Buttons

NOTE To create the flower pattern as shown, you will need 1 yard (.91m) of white ¼-inch (6mm) ribbon, ½ yard (.5m) of yellow ¼-inch (6mm) ribbon, ½ yard (.5m) of white 1-inch (2.5cm) ribbon, 1 yard (.91m) of yellow 1-inch (2.5cm) ribbon, and 1½ yards (1.4m) of green 1-inch (2.5cm) ribbon.

INSTRUCTIONS

Cut six strips of ¼-inch (6mm) white ribbon, each 5 inches (13cm) long. Cut three strips of ¼-inch (6mm) yellow ribbon, each 5 inches (13cm) long. Cut three strips of 1-inch (2.5cm) white ribbon, each 3 inches (7.6cm) long. Cut varying lengths of green 1-inch (2.5cm) ribbon for stems.

Lay the apron on a flat surface. Lay out the flower design one flower at a time, using a needle and matching thread to stitch the individual pieces in place as you go.

Sew a button in the center of each flower.

Machine-stitching is also an option.

DESIGN TIP Although this apron was designed with a floral motif, there are plenty of other options available. For starters, you can embellish your apron with bows, using one of the techniques described on pages 112–113. You can also use a stripe or plaid pattern. Experiment to arrive at your own design. That's half the fun.

SHELF LINERS

Shelf liners are exactly the sort of little luxury that can turn a mundane task, like putting away dishes, into a secret pleasure. When looking for ribbon to line your kitchen shelves, keep in mind the color of the cabinet and your dishes, and look for a patterned or solid ribbon that provides a pleasing contrast.

MATERIALS

Two or more kinds of coordinating ribbons in a variety of widths

Scissors

Glue gun or double-sided tape

Pinking or scallop shears

NOTE The quantity of ribbon you need will depend on the dimensions of your shelf. Before buying ribbon, use a cloth tape measure to determine the width of each shelf or area you want to line.

INSTRUCTIONS

Choose an assortment of ribbons that coordinate with the color of the cabinets and the things you have stored there.

Cut the ribbon to fit the face of the shelf.

Fix it in place with hot glue (permanent) or double-sided tape, which is easier to remove and allows you to easily change the design should you grow tired of it.

DETAIL TIP

Why stop at simply edging the front of your shelves? Follow my lead and, for a nice surprise, line the inside of your cabinets, too! Vertical bands of grosgrain in a contrasting color help dishes stand out. Another trick: For a softer edge, trim ribbon with pinking or scallop shears.

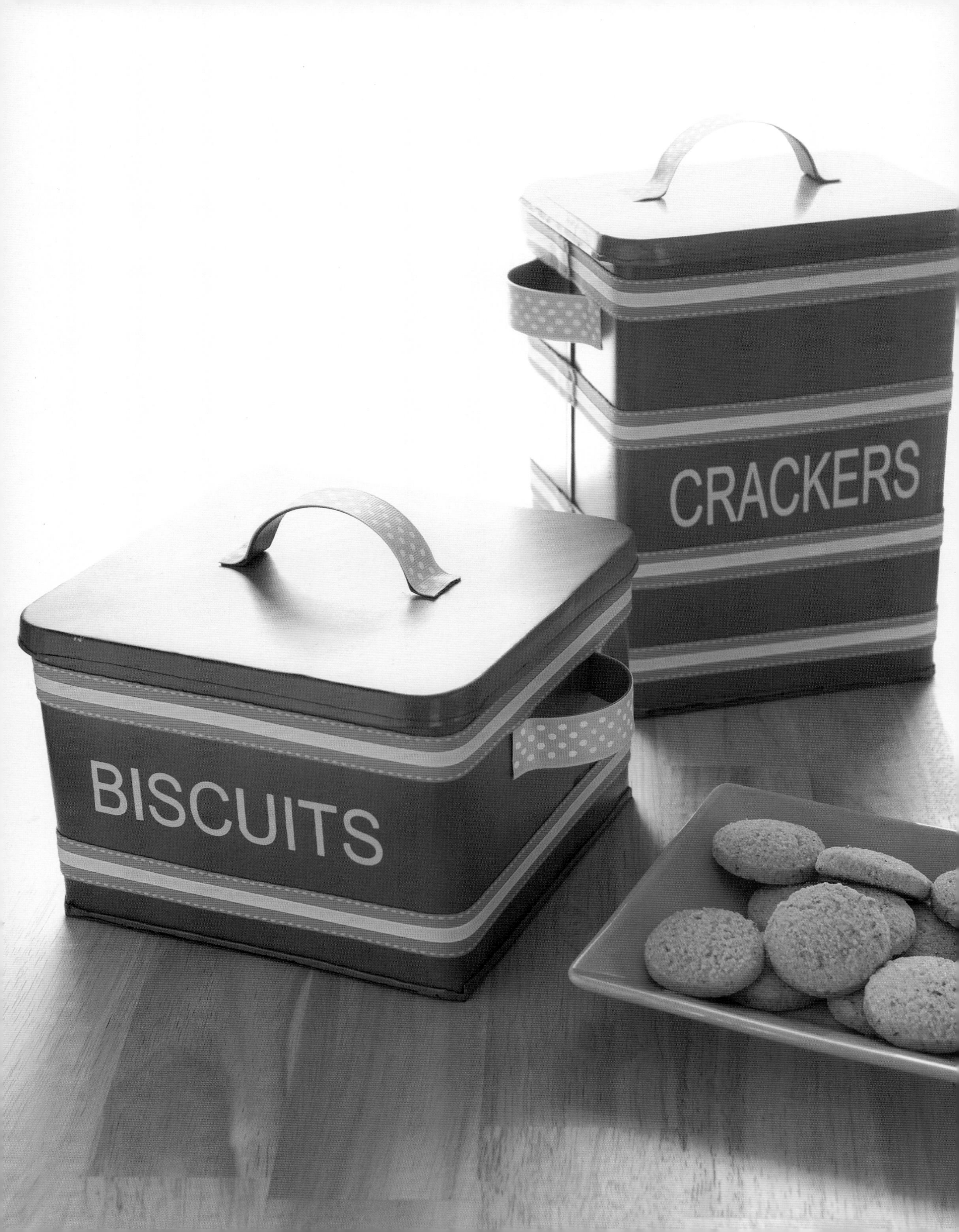
CRACKERS
BISCUITS

CANISTERS

Canisters are an easy way to store staples like crackers and cookies in the open so they're accessible. And because these simple storage devices are front and center, you'll want them to be attractive. To that end, decorate your basic containers with a pleasing ribbon pattern.

MATERIALS

Canister set

Ribbons of varying widths

Scissors

Sealah tape

Burnishing tool

NOTE The quantity of ribbon required will depend on the sizes of the canisters and the pattern you choose.

INSTRUCTIONS

Choose containers to be covered. I found the ones shown left at an antiques store, but you can find similar designs in the kitchen section of most discount and department stores.

Select a variety of ribbons that complement both the color of the canisters and your kitchen's décor.

Apply ribbons to the containers in an eye-catching graphic design, using Sealah tape and the burnishing tool. If you aren't sure where to begin, let the shape of the canisters guide you. Because these canisters had writing on them, I chose to wrap them in simple bands of orange 1-inch (2.5cm) ribbon with yellow ¼-inch (6mm) ribbon layered on top. I also covered the handles in yellow 1-inch (2.5cm) polka-dot ribbon.

HELPFUL TIP When wrapping an object with multiple strands of ribbon, maintain a neat and tidy look by starting and ending each strand in the same place. For these kitchen canisters, I started and stopped each band of ribbon at the canister's metal seam.

DISH TOWELS

Dish towels are synonymous with dish duty and other less-than-glamorous kitchen chores. But add a large graphic design, like the grosgrain daisy shown left, to the towel's face, and the drudgery disappears. In its place: an eye-catching work of art.

MATERIALS

Ready-made dish towels in colors that coordinate with your kitchen's décor

Ribbon in a variety of widths and colors that coordinate with the towels

Sewing needle

Thread that coordinates with ribbon

Buttons

Sewing machine

NOTE To copy my flower design, you will need ½ yard (.5m) each of 1-inch (2.5cm) and ¼-inch (6mm) orange ribbons, and ⅔ yard (.6m) each of 1-inch (2.5cm) yellow polka-dot ribbon and ¼-inch (6mm) cream ribbon. Stems can be made from 1½ yards (1.4m) of ½-inch (13mm) green ribbon.

INSTRUCTIONS

Fold the towel in thirds with the center section facing out.

Lay out a pattern in the center section of the towel, as this will allow for maximum exposure of your design.

Once you've settled on a motif, use the sewing machine to attach the ribbon to the face of the towel.

NOTE Complicated patterns can be affixed to towels with Sealah tape; however, for results that will stand up to multiple washings, sewing is recommended.

EASY TIP For a clean and simple look, limit your design to a 2-inch (5cm) ribbon band along the bottom edge of the towel. Instead of a solid ribbon, spice things up with a patterned design or layer several ribbons.

ISLANDS

Kitchen islands provide extra storage and workspace, which can be very helpful in a room that today has become the hub of the house. Personalize your island with a few grosgrain embellishments. Here, I outlined the top of mine in a jaunty yellow, orange, and green stripe and the drawers in solid green.

MATERIALS

Ribbon

Sealah tape

Burnishing tool

Foam paintbrush

Mod Podge or polyurethane

INSTRUCTIONS

Determine which areas of your kitchen island you'd like to highlight.

Measure the island and cut ribbon to fit.

Use Sealah tape and the burnishing tool to adhere ribbon to the island's surfaces.

To make cleanup easy, seal the ribbon with Mod Podge or polyurethane.

DESIGN TIP
Don't limit your embellishments to the island itself. Storage baskets and other containers that are stowed on the island can also be decorated. Here, I trimmed the liners of my storage baskets with a band of 2-inch (5cm) striped ribbon.

Dining by Design

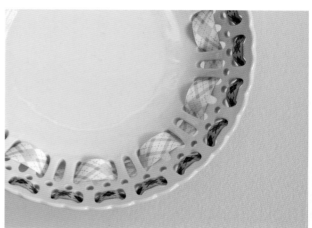

NAPKINS AND PLACE MATS • VOTIVES

DINING ROOMS, BY THEIR VERY purpose, lend themselves to ribbon-embellished furnishings. This is, after all, a room that's all about being sociable and merry. Start with the table linens. Enhance a set you already own, or start with something new. Today there are plenty of affordable, but well-crafted, options available at both discount and department stores. Look for linens in colors that coordinate with the rest of the furnishings in the room—not just your china pattern. Solid colors are the easiest to design with, as they look good with any patterned ribbon. What's more, you don't have to stop at one set. You also don't have to stop at linens. You can

add grosgrain to your seating. Mine is slip-covered, so I simply removed the covers and stitched ribbon across the bottom edge. But you could add it in any number of ways to a wood chair with a drop-in seat. When you're ready, test the waters with a dinner party and gauge the reactions of your guests. If they're anything like my family and friends, they'll soon be asking you to craft these supersimple creations for their own tables.

NOTE Dining rooms are prone to messes and spills, especially on linens. So test ribbons for color-fastness (see page 116). Anything that needs cleaning should be sewn or secured with Sealah tape.

VOTIVES

Votives are an easy way to add sparkle to the dining experience. Ribbon not only turns these inexpensive candleholders into one-of-a-kind creations, it also helps the candlelight cast a subdued, but colorful, glow.

MATERIALS

2½-inch (6cm) tall glass votive candleholders

Ribbon in two colors

Dimensional silicone

Small paintbrush

NOTE The amount of ribbon you need depends on the size of the candleholder being covered. Each of the votives shown here use approximately ⅔ yard (.6m) of pink ribbon and ⅔ yard (.6m) of green ribbon, both cut in 2½-inch (6cm) strands.

INSTRUCTIONS

Wrap the votive with one color of ribbon, leaving equal space between individual ribbon strands.

Fill in the open spaces with the second color of ribbon, overlapping the edges of the first.

Stick the ribbon to the glass with dimensional silicone, a heat-resistant adhesive that dries clear and adheres easily to smooth surfaces, like glass.

Simply brush the silicone on the back of the ribbon and press it onto the outside of the votive holder.

NOTE Use silicone sparingly so that it doesn't bleed or show through the ribbon.

QUICK TIP

With dimensional silicone, you can apply grosgrain to any glass object—even mirrors. Once you've laid out your pattern, apply glue sparingly and press the ribbon onto the glass.

VINTAGE CHANDELIERS

Vintage chandeliers imbue a room with a magic that new models simply can't provide. Giving them a fresh coat of paint and adding colorful patterned shades dressed with ribbons in contrasting colors will personalize the look. Before hanging your chandelier, inspect the wire. If it's wrapped in cloth or frayed around the edges, be sure to have it rewired first.

MATERIALS

Chandelier

Chandelier shades

Ribbon

Sealah tape

Scissors

INSTRUCTIONS

Choose your chandelier. If it's worn in appearance, that's OK. It's easy to spruce up a metal fixture with paint.

Select ribbons that coordinate with the colors in the room and the color of the chandelier.

Ribbons can be wrapped around the arms and base of the fixture; they can also be used to trim the shades.

Before wrapping the ribbon, line the area with a strip of Sealah tape. This will ensure that the ribbon stays in place while the chandelier is hanging.

RIBBON TIP

Grosgrain not only comes in a wide array of colors, widths, and patterns, it is available in flat and pleated styles. Pleated grosgrain is perfect for trimming the base of lampshades. Don't worry if you can't find the color that you are looking for. Plain grosgrain can be pleated as well. Simply follow the instructions on page 114.

PLATES

Plates don't have to be restricted to the top of the table. They can also be used to decorate your dining room walls. Pierced designs, like those shown here, are perfect for weaving ribbon in and out of the lacelike pattern. The ribbon also serves as a hanging device for the plate.

MATERIALS

Plates with lacelike-patterned edges in a variety of sizes

Ribbon in widths that can be easily threaded through the openings in the plates

Scissors

INSTRUCTIONS

Look for plate designs with holes that are wide enough to accommodate ribbons that are at least ¼-inch (6mm) wide. Anything smaller will not show. Craft and antique stores are two good sources.

Weave ribbon in and out of the openings, leaving enough at each end to tie a loop for hanging. The knot will also ensure that the ribbons stay in place for as long as the plate is hanging.

HELPFUL TIP

Before hanging plates on the wall, take time to think about their arrangement. If you have trouble visualizing how they will look, trace the outline of each plate on brown mailing paper, cut out, and tape these paper "plates" to the wall. Once you've arrived at an arrangement that you like, replace your paper plates with the real thing.

DINING CHAIRS

Dining chairs come in a variety of styles and offer a comfortable way for guests to gather around the table. Simple upholstered seats take on a sophisticated look with the addition of a skirted slipcover. Give the cover some contemporary cachet by outlining the skirt's pleats with grosgrain in a contrasting color. The look can be followed through on both the seat and the back of the chair.

MATERIALS

Parson-style dining chairs

Brown mailing paper

Fabric

Sewing machine

Thread in color that coordinates with fabric

Ribbon

Scissors

NOTE The amount of fabric and ribbon you need will depend on the size of your chair. Each of the covers shown left uses approximately 3 yards (2.7m) of fabric and 13 yards (12m) of contrasting grosgrain ribbon.

INSTRUCTIONS

Make a paper template of your chair's upholstered body, adding ¼-inch (6mm) to each side for a seam allowance. To make the tracing process easier, lay the paper on a large flat surface, then lay the chair on the paper. Trace the side. Rotate the chair and repeat.

Pick a fabric that works with the overall look of your room and cut according to the pattern.

Turn the panels so right sides are facing and pin them together, making sure the seams match up. Sew them together, adding one side at a time.

Turn them right side out and frame the pleats with ribbon.

If sewing is not your forte, there are a variety of ready-made covers available from companies like Sure Fit that can be purchased and dressed up with ribbon.

COLOR TIP When selecting fabric for your chair covers, consider not only the other colors and patterns in the room, but also those of your tableware and linens. This will give the finished room a complete, coordinated look.

All Decked Out

A FEW NOTES ABOUT WEARABILITY AND WASHABILITY

Even though grosgrain is washable, how well it holds up in the wash depends on how it's applied and whether or not it's colorfast. Always test for colorfastness before adding grosgrain to an existing article of clothing. If in doubt, wash the ribbon once before proceeding any further. If the color bleeds into the water or fades, that ribbon isn't the best choice. Sealah tape is machine washable; however, if an article of clothing is going to be washed every week, sewing the ribbon to the fabric may be a better option.

CANVAS SNEAKERS • COTTON HATS • TOTE BAGS

BRACELETS · BELTS · NECKLACES

GROSGRAIN NOT ONLY HELPS brighten up a dull room, it can also work wonders on your wardrobe. My closet is overflowing with ribbon belts that I wear with everything from jeans to suits. And though I'm not partial to hats, I do own a few simply because the brim is trimmed with ribbon. I've become so obsessed that even my watchband and key ring are made of grosgrain. And that's my point. Like trim on a pair of plain panel drapes, a band of colorful ribbon can make the most ordinary pair of sneakers or a basic tote bag feel special. Bracelets, necklaces, even pins also benefit from grosgrain's peppy charms. For example, the color and texture of the ribbon can lend a lighthearted quality to jewelry, which is appealing to young and old alike. But what I really like about accessories made from ribbon is that you can never have too many. As long as you have room to store them, you can keep adding to your collection. What better way to experiment with all the new and wonderful ribbons that come out each season!

CANVAS SNEAKERS

Canvas sneakers are a staple in most kids' wardrobes. And although they are available in a wide assortment of colors, they are often void of flair. Ribbon to the rescue: Use it in place of ordinary white laces and to create punchy patterns that can decorate the front and sides of the shoe. Buy several pairs and experiment with different geometric and abstract designs using a variety of solid and patterned ribbons.

MATERIALS

Canvas sneakers

Ribbon

Scissors

Sealah tape

Burnishing tool

NOTE The amount of ribbon required to complete one pair of sneakers depends on the pattern you choose to create. For the flower design shown at right, 1 yard (.91m) of ribbon was used for the laces and ½ yard (.5m) of ribbon for the flower.

INSTRUCTIONS

Take out the white shoestrings from a pair of sneakers and replace them with grosgrain ribbon "laces" of the same length as the shoestrings, knotting the strings at the end to prevent fraying.

Next, determine the pattern that you want to put on the sneakers and use Sealah tape and the burnishing tool to attach. The exception is polka dots, which cut and apply more easily when backed with Peel 'n' Stick adhesive.

DESIGN TIP Since the surface area for embellishing shoes is limited, this is a good way to make use of small scraps of ribbon. Other shapes, like triangles, squares, and diamonds, can also be used effectively.

COTTON HATS

Cotton hats are classic summer accessories. Ribbon flourishes lend a playful, carefree look. Since ribbon is so easy to add, there's no reason you can't embellish all your hats with a grosgrain twist.

MATERIALS

Cotton fisherman-style cap
or other sun hat

Ribbon in coordinating colors

Sealah tape

Burnishing tool

Glue gun

Scissors

INSTRUCTIONS

The easiest way to add ribbon to a plain hat is to wrap the hatband with a simple strand held in place with Sealah tape.

But don't stop there. Experiment with other ideas. Medallions and rosettes (instructions on page 112) can be turned into flowers and secured to a hat with hot glue. Covered buttons and bows can also be added.

STYLE TIP Assess the shape of your hat and how it sits on your head before deciding where to place your embellishments. Designs show up best when placed on the crown of a hat.

TOTE BAGS

Tote bags come in a variety of sizes and are ideal for carrying everything from groceries to library books. To make these necessary tasks more cheerful, trim your bag with an assortment of solid and patterned ribbons. Layering the ribbons will give the bag a more interesting and stylish look.

MATERIALS

Canvas tote bag

Ribbon in several colors

Scissors

Sealah tape

Burnishing tool

INSTRUCTIONS

Devise a pattern (or several) to fit the shape of the bag and attach the ribbon to the bag with Sealah tape and the burnishing tool. Don't be shy. The more patterns and layers you use, the more distinctive the bag.

When laying out the ribbon pattern for these totes, I followed the architecture of the bag, layering patterned and solid ribbons in a vertical fashion that mirrored the shape of the handle.

QUALITY TIP

For long-lasting totes, I prefer L. L. Bean's canvas bags. Their sturdy construction is great for carrying heavier items. On the other hand, if you want to stitch your design, try a bag made from a lighter-weight material, like cotton, which can easily accept a needle. And don't think that your designs must be limited to utilitarian totes. You can also dress up a small fabric purse with a flirty, feminine design.

BRACELETS

Bangle bracelets created from wooden rings wrapped in ribbon make for fashionable accessories that give any outfit a youthful appearance. For a more dynamic look, pair several ribbons on the same ring. For added interest, wear several at the same time.

MATERIALS

Wooden rings or old bracelets

Ribbon

Sealah tape

Scissors

NOTE The amount of ribbon you need will depend on the size of the ring that's being covered. For the bracelets shown left, I used approximately 3 yards (2.7m) on each.

INSTRUCTIONS

Affix 4 inches (10cm) of Sealah tape at one end of the ribbon and begin wrapping the ribbon around the ring. As you wrap, pull the ribbon tight to maintain a clean look.

When you reach the last 4 inches (10cm) of ribbon, add a second strip of Sealah tape and finish wrapping.

FASHION TIP Why stop with one bracelet? The more, the merrier, I say. Wear several in contrasting colors for a fun, lighthearted look. They even look great on a dressing table piled in a bowl or on a tray.

BELTS

Believe it or not, belts can be made from materials other than leather. Here sturdy grosgrains in a variety of snappy striped patterns are combined to create a fashion-forward accessory. But don't think that all your belts have to be striped. Grosgrain can also be found in an assortment of patterns.

MATERIALS

Ribbon

Pins

D-rings sized to fit the width of your ribbon (they're available from about ⅝ inch [16mm] to 1¼ inches [3.2cm] wide)

Sewing machine

Thread in color that coordinates with primary color in ribbon

INSTRUCTIONS

Measure your waist or hips, depending on where you want the belt to sit, and add 10 inches (25cm).

Cut the ribbon to twice this length, then fold it in half and pin its sides together. (An alternative idea for a reversible belt: Cut two ribbons of different patterns exactly the length you need and pin them together.)

Starting at the folded edge, stitch neatly all the way around the perimeter of the ribbon, staying as close to the edge as possible.

Thread the cut end of the ribbon through the D-rings; fold the cut edge under ¼ inch (6mm), then fold down about ¾ inches (19mm) to cover the D-rings, securing them snugly but not tightly.

Stitch across the ribbon width to enclose the D-rings.

CONSTRUCTION TIP

Your waist measurement is important, but so is the width of the belt loops you plan to put the ribbon through. To make sure the belt you make fits, slide several widths of ribbon through the loops on the pants or skirt your belt will most often be worn with. The size that moves the most easily without catching or leaving a gap between the top of the loop and the edge of the ribbon is the one you want to use.

NECKLACES

Necklaces are an easy way to add color and interest to any outfit and can be crafted from a variety of materials, including beads, spools, and rings. The only rule: Let your creativity run wild. After all, isn't it fun to have an original piece of jewelry?

MATERIALS

Several sizes of beads, spools, and rings

Ribbon in varying widths

Sewing needle

Thread in color that coordinates with ribbon

Scissors

INSTRUCTIONS

Lay out beads and ribbons and begin threading beads from the center of the ribbon, working toward each end. Add knots between the beads to maintain even spacing. Spools wrapped with ribbon may be substituted for beads.

One alternative is to make a necklace from rings and ribbon. First, lay one ring on a work surface. Lay a second ring on top of the first, overlapping the two by ½ inch (13mm). Thread the ribbon under the first ring and over the second and back under the first. Lay a third ring on top of the second and repeat. Keep going until the necklace is the length you want.

CREATIVE TIP Instead of creating a necklace from scratch, why not restring a favorite set of beads or shop garage sales and flea markets for old necklaces that can be restrung in a variety of ways? Once you have one of these clever necklaces, you will be eager to make more.

RIBBON NOTES & RESOURCES

WHETHER YOU ARE A RIBBON NOVICE OR a crafter with years of experience, you'll have more fun creating the projects in this book if you first take the time to gather all the necessary supplies and learn a few ribbon-working techniques. That's precisely the point of this section. Here you'll find descriptions of basic supplies, tips for working with grosgrain, and a listing of my favorite resources for ribbons, fabrics, supplies, and furnishings. And because the uses for grosgrain are practically limitless, I've also included some additional thoughts on making this wonderful embellishment part of your everyday experience.

The beauty of the projects in this book lies in the fact that all can be completed with a few simple tools, many of which you may already own. Those you don't are readily available by mail or at your local hardware or craft supply store. Once you have gathered all the necessary equipment, create a central storage location. This can be a simple plastic box or a cabinet outfitted with bins for sorting cutting tools, adhesives, measuring devices, sewing equipment, and drawing tools. While a sewing machine is recommended for certain projects (slipcovers, pillows, and anything that will be tossed in the wash multiple times), it's not required. There are alternatives to sewing that will yield similar results, and I have given instructions for these in the pattern instructions.

ADHESIVES

ALEENE'S NO-SEW FABRIC GLUE

This easy-to-use adhesive bonds fabric for a permanent hold until washed. For this reason, I don't recommend its use for adding ribbon to things like table linens or clothing articles that must be washed. I do, however, advocate using this glue for applying fabric and ribbon to lampshades (it dries clear), pillows, and other items that won't come into contact with water.

DIMENSIONAL SILICONE

This clear, translucent glue is made specifically to work with glass. It's also resistant to heat, making it the ideal substance for adhering ribbon to glass candleholders. (Allow the silicone to set for twenty-four hours before burning a candle in the holder.) For best results, wash and dry glass first, as glue adheres best to a clean surface. Also use it sparingly, so the glue doesn't bleed through the ribbon.

DOUBLE-SIDED TAPE

This office-store staple is perfect for loosely bonding ribbon to a variety of surfaces, including furniture and walls. Use it while you are experimenting with various pattern options or for temporary treatments, like a ribbon table cover that will only be in place for a dinner party or two. Scotch is my brand of choice, as it doesn't leave sticky marks behind when removed from painted surfaces.

MOD PODGE

Billed as the original "all-in-one" sealer, this water-based glue dries clear and holds tight, making it the perfect sealer for wood, paper, fabric, ribbon, and other porous materials. Mod Podge is also nontoxic and cleans up with soap and water, making this one kid-friendly, all-purpose glue. Finish choices include high gloss, matte, and shiny, which has a hint of sparkle. For an ultrasmooth look, lightly sand between coats.

PEEL 'N' STICK

Sold in sheets, Peel 'n' Stick is a strong, all-purpose, double-sided adhesive. I've found that it works great for cutting shapes like polka dots, as it prevents the edges from fraying. Like double-sided tape, Peel 'n' Stick can be used to affix ribbon to walls or furniture. The difference is that the Peel 'n' Stick bond is more permanent than double-sided tape and it's not always as easy to remove.

SEALAH TAPE

Sold on rolls and in a variety of widths, this double-sided, pressure-sensitive adhesive holds like glue without the mess. The width of your ribbon determines the width of tape you need to use. For example, use ½-inch (13mm) Sealah with ½- to ¾-inch (13 to 19mm) wide ribbon. And, unlike glue, Sealah tape is washable, and because it's both acid- and lignin-free, it will not yellow over time, changing the color of your ribbon.

BURNISHING TOOL

This rollerlike tool is perfect for flattening and pressing ribbon. Use it whenever Sealah tape is required to set the bond between ribbon and adhesive, permanently fixing the ribbon in place. Burnishing tools come in different sizes and weights, so you can easily match the one you are using to the width of your ribbon and the weight of the material.

GLUE GUN

There are dozens of glue guns on the market—from small 4-inch (10cm) models to heftier 8-inch (20cm) types. Before you buy, test-drive a few models: Hold them in your hand and see how they feel. You want something that is comfortable to hold and easy to operate. My favorite model has a removable plug that makes it cordless, and thus much easier for you to maneuver.

STAPLE GUN

An all-purpose staple gun is perfect for decorating projects, such as stretching ribbon around a board, small upholstery jobs, or adding grosgrain trim to a shelf. Staples come in various weights and should be matched to the material you are fastening. For example, a lightweight ribbon should not be attached with a heavy-duty staple.

MEASURING TOOLS

If a straight edge is what you want, the best material to use for measuring is metal. A cloth tape measure yields the most accurate measurements when working with soft goods and upholstered furniture. The reason: The tape's flexible nature can easily follow the shape of the piece you are measuring—yielding more accurate dimensions.

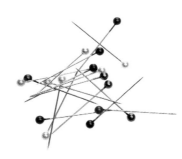

PINS

An essential tool, straight pins help temporarily hold two objects together. This makes it easier for you to cut a straight line, add a length of ribbon to a lampshade, or sew together two panels of fabric to create a pillow. The best pins have large, bulbous heads that not only allow for easy grasping, but also let you clearly see the location of the pin.

SCISSORS/X-ACTO KNIFE

Scissors are one tool essential for every ribbon project. Of course, there are many kinds of scissors to choose from. A good, basic scissors is one that cuts a clean, sharp line without tearing at the fabric or ribbon. Specialty scissors, like pinking or scallop designs, can be used to give ribbon a decorative edge—perfect for shelf treatments. When scissors cannot be used, an X-acto knife can do the trick. With these ribbon projects, I used it primarily to score the back side of my polka dots, making the protective backing on the Peel 'n' Stick paper easier to remove.

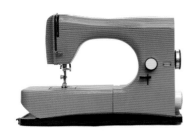

SEWING MACHINE

A sewing machine is not necessary to complete most projects in this book, but it does come in handy when you're attaching ribbon to things that will receive a lot of wear and tear or heavy-duty washing on a regular basis. A sewing machine can also be used for creating slipcovers and some of the other soft furnishings used in this book (though it's not necessary, since ready-made items do exist).

THREAD

When you sew with thread, it creates a permanent bond between ribbon and fabric and allows your project to go in the wash, making it an ideal solution for finishing things like napkins that will be washed over and over again. When selecting a thread for a project, choose a color that closely resembles the main color in the ribbon or fabric that you are sewing.

BASIC TECHNIQUES

Though some of the projects in this book may seem a bit complicated, take heart. They're not. In fact, most of the projects can be completed using the few basic ribbon-working techniques outlined below. Taking time to learn these tricks before you begin will make the crafting process go much more smoothly. Making bows requires few tools, little time, and minimal skill. What's more, they can dress up everything from lampshades to hats.

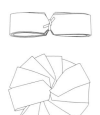

ROSETTE

This fanciful pom-pom-like bow looks great on box lids, canister tops, and other containers.

Start with 1 yard (.91m) or more, depending on how full you want your rosette to be, of 1-inch (2.5cm) ribbon. Hold four fingers on one hand together and wrap with the ribbon. The fullness of the bow will depend on how many times you wrap it around your fingers. Slide the ribbon off your fingers and pinch it together at the center. Cut a notch through the layers on each side. Tie a piece of thread the same color as the ribbon around the center cuts, pull thread taut, and knot. To form the pom-pom shape, spread the loops outward and twist, shaping them into a fluffy ball.

MEDALLION

Pleating grosgrain ribbon into medallions results in a pinwheel shape that's intricate, yet sturdy, and can be used to give your wardrobe or décor a little fashion-forward flair.

Select ribbons and cut in 12-inch (30.5cm) to 24-inch (61cm) strands (the longer the strand, the bigger the medallion). Make a series of accordion folds in the strand, holding the folds in place with your fingers while you work. Finish with both ends of the ribbon facing the same direction. Thread a needle and knot it, leaving a 1-inch (2.5cm) tail. Pass the needle and thread through the layers ¼ inch (6mm) from the selvedge edge. Bring the ends of the thread together; knot close to the ribbon. Cut off the excess thread. Glue the ends of the ribbon together, covering the knot. Adjust the folds so they're evenly spaced. Press the center of the bow to flatten it, rotating the folds in one direction.

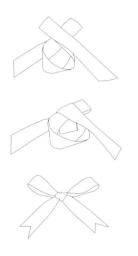

SINGLE BOW

Often seen wrapped around packages, this classic adornment has cheery loops and long tails.

Start with a minimum of 12 inches (30.5cm) of ribbon. If you're adding a bow to a package, you will first need to wrap ribbon around the box and knot it before beginning the steps below. Create two evenly sized loops, one at each end of the ribbon. Cross the right loop over the left. Knot the loops by threading the right loop behind the left, under and up through the hole; make sure the ribbon is not twisted or bunched. Pull the loops tight, creating a smooth knot. Adjust the loops and trim the ribbon tails to the desired length. To keep the ends of the bow from fraying, cut the tails in the shape of a V by folding the ribbon in half and cutting on the diagonal from corner to fold.

DOUBLE BOW

A fresh take on the classic single bow, this easy adornment provides twice the decorating punch.

Start with a minimum of 24 inches (61cm) of ribbon. Tie a single bow with tails that are equal in length. Don't finish the ends of the bow; you'll need them to make the second one. Here's how: Position the single bow horizontally. Make a loop of each tail. Cross the top loop (the one that exits the knot of the existing bow at the top) over the bottom one, under and through the hole; make sure the ribbon is not twisted or bunched. Pull loops to tighten, making sure the knot of the second bow overlaps the knot of the first. Trim the tails in the shape of a V.

WINGED BOW

This decorative knot can add a sophisticated touch to the simplest of projects. Use it to dress up picture frames, mirrors, even a doorknob.

Unless you are wrapping ribbon around a package or another object, you will only need 12 to 14 inches (30.5 to 35.5cm) of ribbon to make this bow. Begin by crossing the left tail over the right. Knot by threading the left tail behind the right one, under, and up through the hole. Pull evenly on the tails until the ribbon has tightened into a clean, smooth knot. Arrange the folds and trim the ends of the ribbon.

MAKING PLEATED GROSGRAIN

You can buy pleated grosgrain at most trim shops. The problem is that the color range is often limited to basic shades of white, blue, and other primary hues. If you are unable to find a ready-made pleated ribbon in the color you crave, you can make your own. Here's how:

Decide on the length of pleated ribbon you need to complete your project. For example, if you are adding ribbon to a lampshade, measure the shade's circumference first. Next, decide the width of your pleat. Then, calculate the amount of ribbon required using this formula: Width of pleat x 3 x length of ribbon required.

Cardboard gauges will help keep pleats uniform. To make, cut four strips in half the width of your finished pleat. For example, if you are making 1-inch (2.5cm) pleated ribbon you will need ½-inch (13mm) wide cardboard gauges. For ease of use, make gauges long enough to stick out at the top and bottom of your ribbon.

To pleat ribbon, place one gauge straight across the ribbon ½ inch (13mm) from one end. Fold the ribbon over the gauge and crease the ribbon at the fold. Place the second gauge on the ribbon directly over first, fold the ribbon over the gauge again, and crease the ribbon at the fold. This is the first half of one full pleat.

Turn the ribbon over and form the second half of the pleat by placing the third gauge across the ribbon next to the first fold. Fold the ribbon over the gauge and crease at the fold. Place the fourth gauge on the ribbon directly over the third. Fold the ribbon over the fourth and crease at the fold. The pleat is now complete.

Remove the gauges, and using a knotted double thread tack the two pleats together with a single stitch. Let the needle hang free in back to tack each succeeding pleat. Turn the ribbon and continue until the end of the ribbon is reached. Finish by sewing a line of machine stitches along the top edge of the ribbon and remove the thread used for tacking pleats.

HELPFUL HINTS

The secret to a successfully completed craft project lies in having the proper tools and understanding the necessary techniques. Here are a few time-tested tips for maintaining an orderly work area and a few of my favorite ribbon-working techniques.

STORING RIBBON

Without an organized storage plan, ribbon can unravel into a tangled mess. To keep my ribbons in line, I borrowed an idea from my local trim store. I wrap them around cards with U-shaped notches cut at either end. The advantage to this method is that the ribbon packs flat—an ideal solution if you don't have much space. The downside is that card-wrapped ribbon, if stored for a long time, ends up creased and must be ironed before it is used. Another idea is to wrap your stash around a cardboard tube like those used for bathroom tissue or paper towels. To help keep the ribbon in place, slit the tube about 1 inch (2.5cm) lengthwise and then tuck the tails into the slit. Reusing empty thread or ribbon spools is another option.

A CLEANER CUT

To ensure a crisp edge, always cut grosgrain against a piece of low-tack blue painter's tape. Simply position the tape on the ribbon at the angle you want to cut. The tape edge will also provide a guide for cutting a straight line. Carefully remove the tape once the ribbon is cut.

CREATING A FINE FINISH

Nothing ruins the look of a fabulous ribbon project faster than frayed edges. To eliminate this problem on nonwashable projects, seal the ribbon's ends with a thin layer of craft glue. Here's how: Use a toothpick to apply the glue (I like Aleene's No-Sew fabric glue because it dries clear) to the cut ends of the ribbon. For washable projects, use clear nail polish or a liquid seam sealant, such as Liqui-Fuse.

SEALAH TAPE SECRETS

In reading the instructions for these projects, you will notice that I use Sealah tape in places that would normally require sewing or hot glue. Here's why: Sealah tape, unlike hot glue, is mess free.

It won't drip or bleed through the ribbon. And unlike a stitch, it can be lifted up and reapplied until you have the ribbon positioned precisely where you want it. Here are three easy steps to follow when using Sealah tape:

1. Remove the backing from one side of the tape and press it onto the ribbon.

2. Remove the backing from the second side and position the ribbon.

3. Press the ribbon in place using a burnishing tool to create a strong, smooth bond.

THE COLORFAST TEST

While it's true that most grosgrains are machine washable, it's best not to tempt fate. Before applying ribbon to a washable item, such as a tablecloth, a set of napkins, or an article of clothing, test to make sure the color won't bleed. To do so, cut a small strand from the roll and soak it in water. If the dye runs, the ribbon is not colorfast and should be machine washed before it is used.

OTHER CLEVER USES FOR RIBBON

As you have seen, grosgrain ribbon offers an easy way to add style to your home and accessories. Here are a few quick and easy ideas that can be used to accent the projects in this book:

- Dress up plain curtain panels by adding grosgrain to the inside lead edge or just across the bottom edge.

- Sew ribbons to the open end of a standard pillowcase. Tie them in a bow for a decorative finish. Ribbon ties can also be used to fasten the ends of the duvet instead of buttons.

- Hang pictures or mirrors from strands of grosgrain. Select colors that complement the color of the wall or the colors in the object that you are hanging.

- Use a leftover strand of ribbon to tie back a pair of curtains.

- Ribbon can be functional as well as decorative when it is used to tie panels to the drapery rod.

- Lengths of ribbon can be tied across a window as an alternative to traditional curtains. Varying the ribbon color and length will add interest.

- Ribbons can make effective fastenings for pillows and are easier to sew onto a pillow than inserting zippers or sewing buttons and buttonholes. This will lend a more casual look.

- Punch holes along the top and bottom edges of a plain lampshade and thread with ribbon. You can secure the ends with a bow.

- Rather than putting pictures in frames, simply attach them to lengths of ribbon with double-sided tape or Sealah tape. Tie the top in a bow and hook on a nail.

- Dress up a vase: Tie a bow around the neck of a glass vase and place it on a mantle or table.

- When entertaining, use grosgrain to tie together napkins, menus, or flatware—an especially good idea for buffet-style serving.

- For festive party decorations: Layer ribbons of varying colors and patterns over the top of a white cloth, hang them from a chandelier, drape them around a window frame, or weave them through the backs of slatted chairs and tie in bows.

- Sew or Sealah tape ribbon to vests, jackets, skirts, and other clothing.

TIPS & TRICKS

A few thoughts to make working with grosgrain easier:

- Select a designated work area. When making oversized items, like drapery panels, use an expansive flat surface to save yourself hours of back-breaking bending.

- Sharp scissors are a necessity for making crisp cuts. And never cut ribbons with scissors that you've used on sticky things like tape, as it will never create a clean line.

- If you don't own a burnishing tool, pick up a wall-paper roller at your local hardware store. Use the roller to fuse the ribbon to Sealah tape.

- Always wash fabrics before applying any ribbon. This will help the ribbon adhere to the fabric.

- Iron wrinkled ribbon to remove creases.

- If the object you are adding ribbon to will receive a lot of hard use, attach the ribbon with a needle and thread.

- Use glue sparingly, as it can easily stain ribbon.

- Pull ribbon as tightly as possible when wrapping an object like the leg of a chair. This will give your finished piece a neat appearance.

- To avoid errors and wasted ribbon, always measure twice before cutting ribbon.

- Start with small projects to gain confidence, and then move on to the bigger ones.

SHOP SMART

Antique shops, garage sales, and flea markets are all good sources for material that can be spruced up with ribbon. Here's how to shop successfully:

- Inspect an item before you buy it, but keep in mind that you can always fix wobbles, dated finishes, and scarred surfaces.

- Get creative. Reconsider the function of an item. I used vintage milk glass plates as a wall decoration rather than their expected use of serving food.

- Think outside the box. Shop for supplies in unexpected places. Beyond the usual hardware, home centers stock a wide array of knobs, feet, casters, moldings, and other items that can be used to enhance a vintage find.

DESIGN LIKE A PRO

Follow these tips to create one-of-a-kind projects:

- Experiment by laying out several ribbon combinations before settling on a final design. The more options you explore, the better your chances of coming up with a truly spectacular design.

- Be surprising in your color choices. Go beyond the usual pairings of red with blue or blue with green. Instead, mix a cool color, like blue, with a warmer color, like orange. Or mix together multiple shades of one color.

- Protect finished projects with Mod Podge or clear polyurethane. Acrylic formulations dry quickly and won't yellow over time.

- Remember, there's no wrong way to use ribbon. Plug in your creativity and enjoy the results.

RESOURCES

Having a good list of resources makes it much easier to complete a project. The following is a list of my favorite stores and websites for finding ribbons, fabrics, tools, and furnishings. If you can't find what you are looking for in a store near you, don't hesitate to order from a website. Many offer swatch services so you can see in advance what the ribbon or fabric you are thinking of buying looks like before you place a final order.

RIBBONS & TRIMS

B & J FLORIST SUPPLY
102 West 28th Street
New York, New York 10001
212-564-6086
Floral supplies, floral paper, ribbon, spray paints, tools such as scissors and glue guns, vases, table decorations, and basic craft supplies.

BELL-OCCHIO
8 Brady Street
San Francisco, CA 94103
415-864-4048
www.bellocchio.com
An extensive selection of exquisite ribbons and craft supplies.

BLACK INK
5 Brattle Street
Cambridge, MA 02138
617-723-3883
www.blackinkboston.com
An eclectic mix of fabric and ribbons.

C. M. OFFRAY AND SONS, INC.
Lion Ribbon
Route 24
P.O. Box 601
Chester, NJ 07930
908-879-4700
www.offray.com
e-mail: questions@offray.com
Supplier of solid and dotted grosgrain ribbons. List of retail distributors available on website.

THE CREATIVE TOUCH
3 East Florida Avenue
Beach Haven Park, NJ 08008
609-492-9092
www.ribbonlady.com
Distributor of Offray and Lion ribbons at wholesale prices. Minimum order applies.

HYMAN HENDLER AND SONS
21 West 38th Street
New York, NY 10018
212-840-8393
www.hymanhendler.com
e-mail: ribbons58@aol.com
Fabulous selection of grosgrains in a wide variety of patterns, colors, and widths.

M & J TRIMMINGS
1008 Sixth Avenue
New York, New York 10018
800-9-MJTRIM
www.mjtrim.com
e-mail: mjtrim.info@mjtrim.com
A stellar selection of grosgrain in a rainbow of colors, plus a vast assortment of buttons and other decorative trims.

MIDORI
708 Sixth Avenue North
Seattle, WA 98109
800-659-3049
www.midoriribbon.com
e-mail: customerservice @midoriribbon.com
A fine selection of grosgrain ribbons in a fresh palette of colors.

MOKUBA LLC

55 West 39th Street
New York, NY 10018
212-869-8900
www.jkmribbon.com
*Distributor of Mokuba ribbons.
Call for retailers.*

THE RIBBONERIE INC.

191 Potrero Avenue
San Francisco, CA 94103
415-626-6184
www.theribbonerie.com
e-mail: theribbon@msn.com
*Carries a wide assortment of
domestic and imported
ribbons.*

THE RIBBON FACTORY

602 North Brown Street
P.O. Box 405
Titusville, PA 16354
866-827-6431
www.ribbonfactory.com
e-mail: ribbon@tbscc.com
*Stocks a wide assortment of
grosgrain ribbons and other
trims.*

THE RIBBONRY

119 Louisiana Avenue
Perrysburg, OH 43551
419-872-0073
www.ribbonry.com
e-mail: info@ribbonry.com
*An unprecedented selection of
ribbons for every style and
occasion.*

RIBBON SHOP

877-742-5142
www.ribbonshop.com
*A great online source for
brand-name solid and striped
grosgrain ribbons.*

SO-GOOD INC.

28 West 38th Street
New York, NY 10001
212-398-0236
*New Yorkers in the know shop
here for all their ribbon needs.
The prices can't be beat.*

THE STORE ACROSS THE STREET

64 West 38th Street
New York, NY 10018
212-354-1242
*The sister shop to Tinsel
Trading.*

STRANO DESIGNS

P.O. Box 896
East Sandwich, MA 02537
508-454-4615
www.stranodesigns.com
*My favorite online source for
preppy grosgrains in a wide
array of colors.*

TINSEL TRADING COMPANY

47 West 38th Street
New York, NY 10018
212-730-1030
www.tinseltrading.com
e-mail: sales@tinsel
trading.com
*Distributor of new and antique
ribbons and trims.*

ARTS & CRAFT SUPPLIES

AC MOORE

www.acmoore.com
*Craft chain with shops
nationwide.*

B & J FLORIST SUPPLY

102 West 28th Street
New York, New York 10001
212-564-6086

THE CHRISTMAS TREE SHOPS

888-327-3232
www.christmastreeshops.com
*An East Coast chain of craft
superstores. Floral supplies,
floral paper, ribbon, spray
paints; tools such as scissors
and glue guns; vases; table
decorations and basic craft
supplies.*

CRAFTOPIA.COM

www.craftopia.com
*The Home Shopping Network's
online source for craft supplies.*

FISKARS BRANDS, INC.

7811 West Stewart Avenue
Wausau, WI 54401
800-950-0203
www.fiskars.com
*Manufacturer of scissors,
edgers, and hand punches.*

HOBBY LOBBY

www.hobbylobby.com
*A nationwide craft supply
chain.*

JO-ANN

www.joann.com
*Craft supplies for all projects.
Shops nationwide.*

JODEE'S INC.

6606 Wilding Place
Riverside, CA 92506
888-888-1899
www.jodeesinc.com
*The only source for Sealah
tape, the two-sided clear
adhesive.*

MICHAELS

800-Michaels
www.michaels.com
*Craft supplies for all projects.
Shops nationwide.*

PEARL RIVER

308 Canal Street
New York, NY 10013
212-431-7932
www.pearlriver.com
*Every imaginable art supply
you might need.*

SAVE ON CRAFTS

www.save-on-crafts.com
*Every craft supply you could
possibly need at deep discount
prices.*

BEADS & BUTTONS

ARTISTIC BEAD

228 Fifth Street, Suite 101
West Des Moines, IA 50265
515-334-0020
http://artisticbead.com
*Stocks a wide assortment of
stones and beads for jewelry
making.*

EYEBEADS AND GEMSTONES

214 Fifth Street
West Des Moines, IA 50265
515-279-9100
*Stocks an exotic assortment of
stones for jewelry making.*

M & J TRIMMINGS

1008 Sixth Avenue
New York, NY 10018
800-9-MJTRIM
www.mjtrim.com
e-mail: mjtrim.info@mjtrim.com

FABRIC STORES & SUPPLIERS

DURALEE

800-275-3872
www.duralee.com
*Supplier of a wide range of
affordable solid and floral
fabrics.*

HANCOCK FABRICS

877-FABRICS
www.hancockfabrics.com
*Fabric and sewing supply chain
with stores nationwide. Stocks
Waverly brand fabrics, which
were used to create many of
the projects in this book.*

JO-ANN

800-525-4951
www.joann.com
*A wide assortment of fashion
and upholstery fabrics.*

KRAVET

800-645-9068
www.kravet.com
*Supplier of a wide range of
fabrics, many by well-known
designers.*

ROBERT ALLEN

800-333-3777
www.robertallendesign.com
*Supplier of fashion-forward
fabrics and furnishings.*

WAVERLY

www.waverly.com
*A wide assortment of
traditional and contemporary
furnishing fabrics. Store locator
available.*

HOME FURNISHINGS

THE CONTAINER STORE
www.containerstore.com
Nationwide chain with ribbon, boxes, containers, and other storage items for the home.

HUNTER DOUGLAS
800-789-0331
e-mail: consumer@hunter douglas.com
www.hunterdouglas.com
Manufacturer of a wide range of custom shades and wood blinds.

JAMIE YOUNG COMPANY
www.jamieyoung.com
Manufacturer of a wide assortment of fashion-forward lighting for the home.

KMART
www.kmart.com
Nationwide chain with a vast assortment of affordable home furnishings.

L.L. BEAN
www.llbean.com
Great selection of sturdy canvas totes.

MITCHELL GOLD + BOB WILLIAMS
135 One Comfortable Place
Taylorsville, NC 28681
828-632-9200
www.mgandbw.com
Fun, affordable selection of upholstery, case goods, and art for the home. Most of the upholstered furnishings pictured in this book came from this company.

PIER 1
www.pier1.com
Nationwide chain of affordable home furnishings stores. Great source for baskets and other decorative containers.

PORCH LIGHT
317 Fifth Street
West Des Moines, IA 50265
515-255-5900
Colorful selection of vintage and new home furnishings.

ROBERT ABBEY, INC.
3166 Main Avenue S.E.
Hickory, NC 28602
828-322-3480
www.robertabbey.com
Manufacturer of fine lighting for the home. Most of the lamps in this book came from Robert Abbey.

RUSSELL+HAZEL
901 3rd Street North
Suite 115
Minneapolis, MN 55401
612-313-2714
www.russellandhazel.com
Great selection of cloth-covered storage boxes and office-organizing supplies.

SURE FIT INC.
Customer Service
6575 Snowdrift Road
Allentown, PA 18106
800-305-5857
www.surefit.net
Good source for affordable ready-made slipcovers.

TARGET
www.target.com
Nationwide chain with a vast assortment of fashionable home furnishings, including collections by such noted designers as Thomas O'Brien and Victoria Hagen.

WEDGWOOD
800-955-1550
www.wedgwood.com
Manufacturer of a wide range of china and glassware, including patterns by Jasper Conran.

WEST ELM
888-922-4119
www.westelm.com
Nationwide chain and catalog of contemporary home furnishings.

As a child living in Davenport, Iowa, John Loecke once saw a picture of Chatsworth House, the ancestral home of the Duke and Duchess of Devonshire in England, and decided that that was where he wanted to live. His encouraging, but pragmatic, mom helped him construct a country house out of cardboard, where the six-year-old would dream about long picture galleries, Chippendale chairs, and palm-filled conservatories. As Loecke grew older, his parents, ever obsessed with finding a bigger, better house, trotted their son from one open house to the next. The aspiring artist brought along a notebook to sketch his favorite rooms; later, he would rearrange his parents' living room to match his drawings.

Fast-forward to college where Loecke studied graphic arts and design, and terrorized his modernist-bent roommates with his colorful outlook on design. After graduation, Loecke moved to New York City to work as an editor/writer/stylist/producer for *House Beautiful* specials and *American Homestyle* (*Homestyle*) and *Parents* magazines.

Today, when not producing shoots or writing design-related articles for a variety of shelter magazines (*Better Homes and Gardens, Country Living, Hamptons,* and *Veranda*), and other publications, he can be found running his eponymous interiors firm: John Loecke Inc. His philosophy? "Banish the beige!" as his idol, the celebrated twentieth-century designer Dorothy Draper, once proclaimed. For an interior by John Loecke Inc. plays off those same sentiments, combining rich color, texture, and pattern to create delightful spaces that pop with personality and life. His interior projects have appeared in such publications as *O at Home, Hamptons, Gotham,* and *House Beautiful,* and he was recently featured on HGTV's program *Small Space, Big Style* and in the *New York Times* Home section. In 2004 *House Beautiful* named Loecke one of America's top up-and-coming interior designers.

Loecke and his partner, Jason Oliver Nixon, split their time between a color-packed row house in Brooklyn and an 1840s-era schoolhouse in New York's Catskill Mountains.

This guide, organized by chapter, lists the ribbon brands and quantites used to complete the projects in this book. And if you've seen anything else you like—from accessories to furntiure—that information is listed here as well.

Living Room (page 12)

Sofa: Dale, Mitchell Gold + Bob Williams
Chair: Carter Wingback, Mitchell Gold + Bob Williams
Vintage Coffee Table: Porch Light
Vintage Side Table: Brimfield Antiques Market
Lamp: Chocolate Double Gourd, Robert Abbey
Drapery Panels: Umbra
Picture Frames: Larson Juhl
Paint: Farrow and Ball

Wood Blinds: Hunter Douglas

COFFEE TABLE (PAGE 16)

1½" (3.8cm) Brown, So-Good
⅞" (2.22cm) Jungle Green, Offray

PILLOW (PAGE 18)

Pillow Fabric: Decorator's Walk
Diagonal Design: ⅞" (2.22cm) Antique White, Offray
Square Design: 1½" (3.8cm)
Pistachio, Offray; ⅞" (2.22cm) Dark Brown with Blue Stitching, Strano Designs

LAMPSHADE (PAGE 20)

Shade Fabric: Decorator's Walk
Trim: ⅞" (2.22cm) Dark Brown with Light Blue Stitching, Strano Designs

CURTAIN PANEL (PAGE 22)

Tabs: 1½" (3.8cm) Brown, So-Good; 1" (2.5mm) Light Brown with Dark Brown Polka Dots, Strano Designs
Vertical Stripe: 2" (5.1cm) Dark Brown with Cream Stripes, Strano Designs
Horizontal Stripes: 1½" (3.8cm) Pistachio, Offray; ⅞" (2.22cm) Dark Brown with Light Blue Stitching, Strano Designs; ⅞" (2.22cm) Light Blue with Dark Brown Stitching, Strano Designs

RUG (PAGE 24)

1½" (3.8cm) Pistachio, Offray
1½" (3.8cm) Dark Brown with Light Blue Stripes, So-Good
1½" (3.8cm) Bluebird, Offray
1½" (3.8cm) Jungle Green, Offray
2" (5.1cm) Brown with Cream Stripes, Strano Designs

SEAT CUSHION (PAGE 26)

Top: 3" (7.6cm) Brown, So-Good; 1½" (3.8cm) Blue/Dark Brown/Cream Stripe, So-Good
Front Edge: Two 1½" (3.8cm) widths pieced together, Jungle Green, Offray; 1½" (3.8cm) Dark Brown/Light Blue Stripe, So-Good

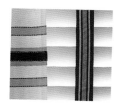

BLINDS (PAGE 29)
½" (13mm) Blue/Dark Brown/Cream Stipe, So-Good

Bedroom (page 30)
Bed: Peabody Slipcovered, Mitchell Gold + Bob Williams
Slipcover: Rain in Sea, Waverly
Night Tables: Lane
Lamps: Small Double Gourd Lamps in Pink, Robert Abbey
Pillow Fabric: Heritage Pear and Heritage Cancun, both Waverly
Duvet Fabric: Heritage Cancun and Gloshen Wedgwood, both Waverly
Paint: Farrow and Ball

BEDDING (PAGE 34)
Sheets and Pillowcases: ⅞" (2.22cm) Baby Maize, Offray; ¼" (6.4mm) Antique White, Offray
Pillow Shams: ⅞" (2.22cm) Antique White, Offray; 1½" (3.8cm) Light Blue/Cream/Dark Blue, So-Good
Blue Decorative Pillows: 1½" (3.8cm) Green/Dark Blue/Cream Stripe, So-Good; ¼" (6.4mm) Antique White, Offray
Green Decorative Pillows: ⅞" (2.22cm) Lemon, Offray; ¼" (6.4mm) Antique White, Offray
Reversible Duvet (green side): 1½" (3.8cm) Blue/Cream/Light Blue Stripe, So-Good
Reversible Duvet (blue side): 1½" (3.8cm) Green/White Stripe, So-Good

HEAD- AND FOOTBOARD COVER (PAGE 36)
1½" (3.8cm) Antique White, Offray
⅞" (2.22cm) Lemon, Offray

NIGHTSTAND (PAGE 38)
1½" (3.8cm) Green/White Stripe, So-Good
1½" (3.8cm) Dark Green/White/Light Green Stripe, So-Good

LAMPSHADE (PAGE 40)
¾" (1.9cm) Green Stripe, Strano Designs
⅞" (2.22cm) Lemon, Offray
⅞" (2.22cm) Green Apple, Offray

BREAKFAST TRAY (PAGE 42)
⅞" (2.22cm) Green Apple Polka Dot, Offray
⅞" (2.22cm) Green Apple, Offray
⅞" (2.22cm) Bluebird, Offray
¼" (6.4mm) Green Apple, Offray
¼" (6.4mm) Bluebird, Offray

PICTURE FRAMES (PAGE 44)
Diagonal-stripe Frame: ¼" (6.4mm) Lemon, Offray; ¼" (6.4mm) Bluebird, Offray; ¼" (6.4mm) Apple Green, Offray
Polka-dot Frame: 1½" (3.8cm) Green Apple, Offray; ⅞" (2.22cm) Centennial Blue Polka-Dot, Offray; ¾" (1.9cm) Green Stirpe, Strano Designs

Rec Room (page 46)

Vintage Table: Porch Light

Chairs: Target

Ottomans: Mo Square, Mitchell Gold + Bob Williams

Fabric for Ottoman Slipcovers: Heritage Cancun

Paint: Farrow & Ball

Linen Boxes: russell+hazel

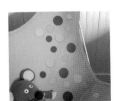

BUTTERFLY CHAIR (PAGE 50)

3" (7.6cm) Royal Blue, 3" (7.6cm) Light Blue, and 3" (7.6cm) Kelly Green, all from So-Good

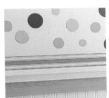

WALL TREATMENT (PAGE 52)

Polka Dots: 3" (7.6cm) Royal Blue, 3" (7.6cm) Light Blue, 3" (7.6cm) Kelly Green, all from So-Good

Stripes: 1½" (3.8cm) Orange/White/Green Stripe and 3" (7.6cm) Light Blue, both So-Good

OTTOMAN (PAGE 54)

1½" (3.8cm) Torrid Orange, Offray

⅞" (2.22cm) Blue/White/Green Stripe, So-Good

GAME (PAGE 56)

Board: 1½" (3.8cm) Blue with Green Stripes and 1½" (3.8cm) Blue with Light Blue Edge, both from So-Good

Pieces: 3" (7.6cm) White/Dark Blue Stripe, 3" (7.6cm) Royal Blue/White Stripe, 3" (7.6cm) Yellow, 3" (7.6cm) Royal Blue, all from So-Good

STORAGE BOXES (PAGE 58)

Polka Dots: 3" (7.6cm) Royal Blue, 3" (7.6cm) Light Blue, 3" (7.6cm) Kelly Green, 3" (7.6cm) Orange, all from So-Good

Stripes: 1½" (3.8cm) Orange Stripe with Polka Dots, 1½" (3.8cm) Blue with Green Stripes, 1½" (3.8cm) Orange/White/Green Stripe, all from So-Good; ⅜" (9.5mm) Yellow Polka Dot/Orange and ⅜" (9.5mm) Orange with Yellow Stitching, both Strano Designs

Kitchen (page 60)

Cabinets: Plain & Fancy

Island: Martha Stewart

Stool: Martha Stewart

Canisters: Porch Light

APRON (PAGE 64)

½" (1.27cm) Green, M & J Trimming

⅞" (2.22cm) Antique White, Offray

⅞" (2.22cm) Maize Polka Dot, Offray

¼" (6.4mm) Maize, Offray

¼" (6.4mm) Antique White, Offray

SHELF LINER (PAGE 66)

1½" (3.8cm) Yellow/Orange/Green Stripe, So-Good

⅜" (9.5mm) Yellow Polka Dot/Orange Stripe, Strano Designs

1½" (3.8cm) Maize, Offray

CANISTERS (PAGE 68)

⅞" (2.22cm) Orange with Yellow Stitching, Strano Designs
¼" (6.4mm) Lemon, Offray
⅞" (2.22cm) Maize Polka Dot, Offray

DISH TOWELS (PAGE 70)

¼" (6.4mm) Green Apple, Offray
⅞" (2.22cm) Maize Polka Dot, Offray
¼" (6.4mm) Antique White, Offray
⅞" (2.22cm) Orange with Yellow Stitching, Strano Designs
⅜" (9.5mm) Orange with Yellow Stitching, Strano Designs

STOOL (PAGE 72)

⅞" (2.22cm) Green Apple, Offray
1½" (3.8cm) Lemon, Offray
⅞" (2.22cm) Maize Polka Dot, Offray
⅜" (9.5mm) Yellow Polka Dot, Strano Designs

ISLAND (PAGE 74)

1½" (3.8cm) Yellow/Orange/Green Stripe, So-Good
⅞" (2.22cm) Green Apple, Offray
Wicker Baskets: 1½" (3.8cm) Green Apple, Offray; ⅞" (2.22cm) Lemon Polka-Dot, Offray

Dining Room (page 76)

Table: Vintage, Brimfield Fleamarket
Chairs: Elmo Slipcovered Side Chair, Mitchell Gold + Bob Williams
Chair Slipcover Fabrics: Decorator's Walk
China: Jasper Conran Chinoiserie White, Wedgwood
Rug: West Elm
Drapery Fabric: F Schumacher & Co.
Paint: Farrow and Ball

NAPKINS AND PLACE MATS (PAGE 80)

Rings: ⅞" (2.22cm) Blue/Green/White Stripes, So-Good
Napkins: 1½" (3.8cm) Green Apple, Offray; ⅞" (2.22cm) Hot Pink, Offray
Fabric: 1½" (3.8cm) Maize Polka Dot, Offray
D-Rings: Jo-Ann

VOTIVES (PAGE 82)

Votive Holders: Jamali Garden Supply
¾" (1.9cm) Green Stripe, Strano
⅞" (2.22cm) Hot Pink, Offray

VINTAGE CHANDELIER (PAGE 84)

Body: ⅞" (2.22cm) and ¼" (6.4mm) Lemon, Offray; ¼" (6.4mm) Shocking Pink, Offray; ⅞" (2.22cm) Pleated Antique White, M & J Trimming

PLATES (PAGE 86)

¼" (6.4mm) Blue/Green, American Crafts Elements, Hobby Lobby
½" (1.27cm) Green/White, American Crafts Elements, Hobby Lobby
¼" (6.4mm) Green/Pink, American Crafts Elements, Hobby Lobby

DINING CHAIRS (PAGE 88)

⅞" (2.22cm) Green Apple, Offray
⅞" (2.22cm) Maize, Offray

Accessories (page 90)

Vintage Tray: Porch Light
Tote Bags: L.L. Bean

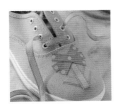

CANVAS SNEAKERS (PAGE 94)

Pink: ⅜" (9.5mm) Green/Orange, American Crafts Elements, Hobby Lobby; ⅜" (9.5mm) Orange with Yellow Polka Dots, Strano Designs
Green: ¼" (6.4mm) Maize, 1½" (3.8cm) Hot Pink, 1½" (3.8cm) Torrid Orange, all from Offray

COTTON HATS (PAGE 96)

Tan: ⅞" (2.22cm) Yellow/Orange/Blue, So-Good; 1½" (3.8cm) Maize, Offray
Yellow: 1½" (3.8cm) Orange Polka Dot, So-Good
Blue: ⅞" (2.22cm) Shocking Pink Polka Dot, 1" (2.5mm) Floral, 1½" (3.8cm) Shocking Pink, all from Offray; ¾" (1.9cm) Green Stripe, Strano Designs
Pink: ⅞" (2.22cm) Pistachio, ⅞" (2.22cm) Shocking Pink, 1½" (3.8cm) Shocking Pink, all from Offray

TOTE BAGS (PAGE 98)

Green: ⅞" (2.22cm) Hot Pink and 1½" (3.8cm) Floral, both Offray; 1½" (3.8cm) Green/White Stripe, 1⅝" (4.1cm) Purple, 1" (2.5cm) Brown Polka Dot, all from Strano Designs
Aqua: 1½" (3.8cm) Shocking Pink, 1½" (3.8cm) Pistachio, ⅞" (2.22cm) Hot Pink, 1½" (3.8cm) Multi-Stripe, all from Offray; ⅞" (2.22cm) Aqua, Decorative Ribbon, Hobby Lobby

BRACELETS (PAGE 100)

Bangles: ¾" (1.9cm) Green Stripe, Strano; ⅜" (9.5mm) Aqua Polka Dot, ⅜" (9.5mm) Purple/Aqua Stripe, ⅜" (9.5mm) Orange Polka Dot, ⅜" (9.5mm) Aqua/Purple/Green Stripe, all from American Crafts Elements, Hobby Lobby
Pins: 1½" (3.8cm) Polka Dots, 1½" (3.8cm) Floral, 1½" (3.8cm) Hot Pink, 1½" (3.8cm) Torrid Orange, all from Offray

BELTS (PAGE 102)

D-Rings: Jo-Ann's
Solid Designs: 1½" (3.8cm) Orange/Green Stripe, 1½" (3.8cm) Brown/Blue Stripe, 1½" (3.8cm) Pink/White Stripe, all from Jo-Anns
Reversible: 1½" (3.8cm) Aqua/Orange Stripe, 1½" (3.8cm) Aqua with Orange Polka Dots, both from Jo-Anns

NECKLACES (PAGE 104)

All Ribbon: Beads, Hobby Lobby; 1½" (3.8cm) Blue/Green Stripe, Strano Designs
Ring: Rings, Hobby Lobby; ⅜" (9.5mm) Blue and Green Polka Dots on White, American Crafts Elements by Hobby Lobby
Ribbon and Bead: Beads, Hobby Lobby; ⅞" (2.22cm) Decorative Ribbon by Hobby Lobby
Spool: Spools and Beads, Hobby Lobby; ⅞" (2.22cm) White Polka Dots, ⅞" (2.22cm) Green Apple, all from Offray

INDEX